John Bell

CAMPING

COOKBOOK

A Complete Guide with Easy and Delicious Recipes

to be Enjoyed in Your Camping Trip

Table of Contents

Introduction

Camping is a great family vacation activity, teaches families about the outdoors and their environment. Camping is a way to enjoy a fun-filled, outdoor adventure safely.The purpose of camping is for fun and relaxation. But to enjoy your trip, it's important to have a basic understanding of safety. Safety is paramount when traveling with children

Camping cooking is a great way to cook outdoors over an open fire. There is no need to worry about charcoal or electrical heaters for cooking your favorite dishes in the woods

Camping is a bit more critical than home cooking because you can't order pizza if anything goes wrong. When you start cooking at the campsite, a little food preparation effort will go a long way. Not only would the meals taste healthier, but they will also be easier to prepare. Before your campsite trip, plan your dinner and snack, and make sure you don't burn your meal or get stuck with chips the first night. The plan will look very different depending on how you camp.

There is no better way than picking up a few things and going out to your ideal camping place to explore the outdoors with family and friends or even alone. It is necessary, though, to ensure that the food and water you intend to use is healthy, whether taken from home or scavenged in the wilderness. The easiest way of making a camping trip goes wrong is to ignore food hygiene. Any vacation can be spoiled by food or water poisoning, which can also contribute to harmful and long-lasting medical problems that you can almost definitely regret.

It's generally better to make some food preparation you'll be doing as safe as possible while camping. To ensure the protection of yourself and the people involved in your party, stop utilizing perishable food products and always use the necessary hygiene procedures. However, the barbecue and cookouts are a favorite of the camping culture. For this purpose, while cooking in the natural surroundings, it is necessary to watch all the appropriate safety precautions for preparing food.

The Need To Practice Proper Food Safety

If adequate safety measures are not taken, many harmful and disease-causing organisms can contaminate the food and drink. Microbiologists have reported more than 200 foodborne illnesses. Many of these infections are contagious and are caused by a combination of viruses, parasites, and bacteria. Hazardous substances and contaminants are also a big source of anxiety and may cause intense disease. The biggest threat for someone who braves the woods is a foodborne disease. For that purpose, the number one safety concern should be food hygiene and food safety.

More caution might be needed, depending on the place, time of year, and other variables. Also, contact municipal officials for any hazards of contamination that might be found in local water sources, as well as for any viruses that are likely to be borne by local wildlife. While enjoying wild game not cooked by a specialist, special caution should be taken. Until prior inspection by a certified food service official, hunters and others in a hunter's group are warned not to consume the wild game.

Keep Cold Food Cold And Hot Food Hot.

It is not necessary to overestimate the value of refrigeration. Over the decades, refrigeration has saved countless lives and is your first protection against food spoiling and inducing disease from microbes, insects, and other creatures. In the first lines of protection against foodborne disease is the propensity to chilled meats and other ingredients. Cold foods often need extra care and must at all times be held at or below 41 degrees Fahrenheit. Food can never be left out for longer than 2 hours, less than an hour if the weather is over 90 degrees F, at room / outdoor temperatures.

It is not very popular to take hot food camping because most hot food consumed outdoors is prepared on a camp stove or open fire, but it does not imply that you are not at risk. In the two-hour cycle following cooking, food cooked in the camp

must be eaten or stored in a colder location.

Choose Foods With Little To No Planning Required.

It sounds gourmet to have a steak or stuffed chicken breast but may create more issues than its value. Canned or pre-packaged foods can make life around the camp simpler and safer. Try canned chicken instead of taking in fresh chicken. For dried noodles and dehydrated vegetables that need just hot water, bring the favorite soup mixes. Several raw food alternatives require immediate planning, and that will decrease the risks of unsafe handling.

Chapter One: Camping Essentials

There is definitely one of the most prominent places on the campsite to enjoy healthy food outdoors. The preparation, ingenuity, and equipment required for creating gourmet meals in the open are not that challenging. Few people say that camping is uncomfortable, frustrating, and may make the food situation particularly stressful. In general, when you camp as quickly as possible, it is simpler to prepare food. Dismay using perishable foodstuffs and always follow the appropriate hygiene measures to safeguard yourself and your mates.

Kitchen Essentials Checklist at Camping

The planning, imagination, and the right equipment for gourmet meals during cooking outdoors are not that difficult. Nice food outside the campsite is one of the greatest. You will enter your campsite with an appendix about what you expect to consume in a forward-looking culture when you were at the campsite.

You just need to feed and rest afterward.

Camping Stove

A camping stove is an important piece of equipment if you are contemplating cooking on your next camping trip. A camping stove for certain cooking types will be required, whether it is a singular or dual burner, cantilevered, or table-top.

Safety is still a concern while cooking, so it's important to take all the appropriate precautions. If you are camping in tents, caravan, or motorhome, it's important not to cook in the unit because of the possible fire danger. Also, poor ventilation can contribute to a build-up of toxic carbon monoxide.

Camping Stove Gas

If you do not have any fuel to start it up, there is no point in keeping a camping stove. Different stoves need various fuel types, but it's safe and convenient to use butane (generally in a blue high-pressure cylinder) or propane (in a red cylinder).

As it is safe and quickly portable, gas is a great complement for cooking fuel. Have a glance at our guide to gas and liquid fuels before using camping petrol.

Dinnerware

It might sound like a given, but it's simple to overlook that you may need to eat and drink something. Since it is safer for the atmosphere than to use single-use paper plates and disposable cutlery, it is worth investing in any reusable dinnerware. Here is what you would need:

- Plates
- Bowls
- Cups
- Mugs
- Forks and knives
- Teaspoons and spoons
- Dishes for Serving

Pots and Pans for camping

You will need certain utensils to cook your meals, whether it's unique camping kitchen appliances or homemade cookware. On the market, there is a broad range of pots and pans available. Custom camping cookware is generally lighter, more durable, and easier to carry. If you plan to cook large quantities for many people, it is necessary to note to carry larger utensils.

Camping Kettle

Packing a kettle can help you have a cup of tea or coffee or cook some pasta or rice. There are many camping kettles on the deal, such as aluminum and stainless steel and rapidly-packable folding kettles. If you're new to camping and have decided to book onto a pitch with electricity, any kettle rated at about 2kw or less will do the job.

Cooking Utensils

No matter which recipe you are trying, you will, at some stage, require knives for slicing, wooden spoons for mixing, and spatulas for tossing. Here is a rundown of what you would need:

- Wooden spoon
- Large spoons
- Tongs
- Spatula
- Whisk
- Sharp knife
- Chopping board

Water Container

It is a concern of comfort to have a complete bottle of water. To refill the container and then use the provision each time you need it, use a tap at your camping site. You can purchase foldable water containers and those with taps from most outdoor stores, which are simple to pack, move, and use.

First Aid Kit

Whenever it comes to camping, protection always comes first. A small first aid kit

is important for every camping trip. When cooking food, burns and cuts are fairly normal, and plasters and bandages may be very helpful.

Here's a list of what you need in the kit:

- A variety of plasters
- Disposable sterile gloves
- A variety of bandages
- Tweezers
- Scissors
- Wipes for cleaning
- Thermometer
- Sticky tape
- Antiseptic cream
- Pain relievers

Folding Toaster For Camping

Affordable, filling, and convenient, toast is an excellent camping meal to eat. There's no reason to carry the toaster with you from home if you have a foldable camping toaster. It's easy, healthy, and great to cook with a camping toaster toasting bread, breakfast sandwiches, and teacakes and melting the cheese in your toast.

Table Camping

You bought all the ingredients, brought all the camping equipment for cooking with you, accompanied a recipe, served it on plates, but where are you planning to eat it? Gather your family or mates around the camping table and make mealtime a shared experience. Camping tables can adapt too; just use the table to arrange a board game or glean everybody round for a game of cards.

Bin Bags

A clean camp is a pleasant camp. Put all the garbage in huge bags and leave

your campsite's area clean and clear; this would decrease the likelihood of predators having an interest and improve the confidence of all in the camp. The camping code of "leave no trace" is crucial to keep in mind, so you can do your hardest to end up leaving your pitch in the same condition as you find it in.

Washing Up Equipment

A healthy routine to fall into is to keep the pitch tidy. Don't encourage washing up to sit around, use the abundant washing facilities, and have a talk with your fellow campers whilst you're at it. It's also a perfect meeting spot. If you don't have the essentials for cleaning up the equipment, the cookware can get dirty. Here is what you would need:

- Washing up liquid
- Towels
- Scouring pad
- Sponge
- Dish-cloth

Storage of Food

You would maintain your food balanced and your atmosphere orderly by using a range of containers. By putting them chilled in Tupperware in your cool box, putting your surplus food in containers, and reusing it the next day, keep your ingredients new. Sheets of beeswax will even help keep food fresh if you don't have any containers.

The Chimney Starter

This foldable compact chimney can make the coal burn in moments without the need for harmful burning lighter fluid, extremely great while using charcoals.

Portable grill

While most campsites have campfires with grates, their state may be less than enticing. It is possible to position this portable grill on top of the campground grill (with collapsing legs) or use it independently (when freestanding). If free camping on public grounds, where there are no grill grates that cover fire pits, may be beneficial.

Thermometer with Quick-Reading

Knowing the precise condition of a slice of meat or the Dutch oven's interior condition may be useful when you're just starting to cook outside. It's easier to know unless you evolve the senses to go through intuition. A perfect method to guess as the steak is done cooking or not is this probe thermometer.

You can actually get away without one if you are new to camping, but it's certainly the key to make things very pleasant.

Cast Iron Skillet With A Lid

This is the camp kitchen MVP. On a camp burner, over a campfire, or snuggled in a bed of charcoal, cast iron may be used. It has an inherently non-stick structure, superior heat preservation, and is essentially indestructible.

Non-Stick Skillet

It is debatable whether or not this is a "necessary" component of camp cooking equipment. Without it, you should get by. But whether you prepare scrambled eggs, pancakes, tuna, or something else that's sensitive, there's no substitution for a decent skillet that doesn't stick. This skillet would last for years if paired with a fitting silicone or wooden spatula.

Dutch Oven

One of the most valuable items of camp cookware that you will own is a Dutch oven. If you can picture it, you can make it in a Dutch oven. Sauté, steam, boil, roast, and bake. A flat rim lid helps you mount charcoals on top, while underneath, you can nestle coals with support legs on the bottom.

Egg Holder

There are many dubious, almost gimmicky camping products out there, but it's worth a plastic egg holder. Before we planned to have one of these, we missed a lot of good eggs.

Streamline

After cleaning your dishes, disinfect against bacteria and viruses, add one of

these tablets to your rinse bucket. It's more potent than old-fashioned chlorine, and on the skin, it's much gentler.

Chapter Two: Breakfast

1. Campfire Breakfast

Preparation time: 20 minutes

Cooking time: 10 minutes

Servings: 5

Ingredients:

- Four large eggs and ½ cup milk
- 1 pound refrigerated hash browns, thawed
- 1 cup chopped ham
- 2 cups shredded cheddar
- ½ tablespoon butter, for greasing the foil

Directions

1. Crack the eggs into a resealable plastic bag and add the milk.
2. Season with salt and pepper.
3. Add the hash browns, ham, and cheese to the bag. Carefully manipulate the bag to combine the ingredients.
4. Butter four squares of aluminum foil.
5. Divide the mixture from the plastic bag between the pieces of foil.
6. Fold it snugly, and seal.

7. Place the packets on a grill or near a campfire, and cook for about 10 minutes.

8. Serve when the eggs are set, and the cheese is melted.

Nutrition*:*

Calories 442, total fat 22 g, carb 35 g, Protein 24 g, sodium 1015 mg

2. Yummy Cobbler

Preparation time: 20 minutes

Cooking time: 10 minutes

Servings: 5

Ingredients:

- 2 ⅓ cups biscuit mix
- ½ cup sweetened almond milk, vanilla flavor
- ½ tablespoon butter, for coating
- 6 fresh peaches, chopped
- 1 cup strawberries, hulled and chopped

Directions

1. Before leaving for camping, combine the biscuit mix and milk in a large, sturdy, resealable bag. Seal the bag.
2. When you are ready to cook, knead the bag with your hands until the ingredients are combined.
3. Butter a large cast-iron skillet.
4. Pour in the fruits, and top them with the batter.
5. Cover the pan snugly with foil, and let it cook over the campfire for about 45 minutes.
6. Once the biscuit topping is no longer doughy, the cobbler is ready.
7. Cool for a few minutes before serving.

Nutrition:

Calories 118, total fat 12.2 g, carb 17 g, Protein 8.1 g, sodium 896 mg

3. Pancakes

Preparation time: 5 minutes

Cooking time: 20 minutes

Servings: 6

Ingredients:

- 2 cups pancake mix, plain
- Water, for mixing
- 1 cup blueberries for topping
- 1 cup bananas for topping
- 1 cup strawberries for topping
- 1 cup whipping cream for topping.

Directions:

1. At home, combine the pancake mix with enough water to make the desired consistency.
2. Pour the batter into a clean condiment bottle, and seal.
3. At the campsite, heat a skillet over the fire or grill.
4. Squeeze some batter onto the pan, cook until bubbles appear, and then flip.
5. When the other side is cooked, serve with the fruit and cream toppings.

Nutrition

Calories 317, total fat 10 g, Carb 63 g, Protein 8.4 g, sodium 898 mg

4. Dutch Oven Scrambled Eggs and Biscuits Recipe

Preparation time: 20 minutes

Cooking time: 10 minutes

Servings: 5

Ingredients:

- 1 large onion, chopped
- 1 bell pepper, chopped
- 4 eggs
- 1 package prepared biscuit dough
- ¼ cup cheddar cheese, grated

Directions

1. Before leaving for camping, in a large bowl, combine the onion, pepper, eggs; whisk well.
2. Pour the mixture into any clean condiment bottle, and seal.
3. Prepare the fire using charcoal coals or wood until the coals are hot enough to cook with.
4. Place the cast-iron Dutch oven on the hot coals, and shift the coals around the oven. Let it sit for a few minutes to heat.
5. Add the oil to the oven and let it get hot. Tip the pot, so the oil coats the bottom.
6. Pour the egg mixture from the bottle into the Dutch oven. Cover, and let it cook for a few minutes.

7. Grease the lid of the oven with a generous amount of oil and spread it evenly.

8. Open the biscuit package and brush both sides of the rolls with vegetable oil.

9. Place the oiled biscuits on top of the greased oven lid.

10. Place the aluminum foil over the top to keep the heat in...

11. Remove the lid once in a while to stir the eggs, and place it back on again.

12. Once everything is cooked, sprinkle cheese on top of the eggs and let it melt.

Nutrition: Calories 256, total fat 16.6 g, Carb 19.2 g, Protein 9.5 g, sodium 353 mg

5. Eggs Benedict Casserole

Preparation time: 10 minutes

Cooking time: 25 minutes

Servings: 5

Ingredients:

- 6 English muffins, cut into small pieces
- 10 ounces turkey bacon, cut into pieces
- 6 large eggs, or 1 cup egg beaters
- 2 cups milk
- Oil spray for greasing

Directions

1. Spray the Dutch oven with oil and set it in the coals to heat.
2. Combine the English muffin pieces with the bacon in the Dutch oven.
3. In a mixing bowl, combine the egg beaters, milk, mustard.
4. Pour this batter on top of the muffin and bacon mixture in the pot, and jiggle the pot, so it soaks in evenly.
5. Let it cook until the eggs are set.
6. Serve, and enjoy.

Nutrition: Calories 302, total fat 9.7 g, Carb 30 g, Protein 23 g, Sodium 866 mg

6. Dutch Oven Eggs Baked in Avocados

Preparation time: 15 minutes

Cooking time: 10 minutes

Servings: 4

Ingredients:

- 4 ripe avocados
- 8 eggs
- Red pepper flakes
- 6 tablespoons hot sauce
- 1 cup salsa

Directions

1. Slice the avocados and remove the seeds. Scoop out enough of the avocado flesh as needed for the egg to fit. Lay the avocados on a flat surface.
2. Crack an egg into each avocado half.
3. Place all the filled avocados into the Dutch oven.
4. Cover the Dutch oven with the lid and place it on the coals for about 15 minutes, rotating every 5 minutes.
5. Serve with hot sauce and salsa.

Nutrition

Calories 377, total fat 32 g, carb 16.4 g, Protein 10.6 g, sodium 758 mg

7. Camp Quiche

Preparation time: 20 minutes

Cooking time: 10 minutes

Servings: 5

Ingredients:

- 6 eggs
- 1 cup broccoli, chopped
- 1 cup mushrooms, chopped
- 1 cup tomatoes, diced
- 1 cup cheddar, shredded

Directions

1. Whisk the eggs in a large mixing bowl, and fold in all the other ingredients EXCEPT the cheese.
2. Pour this mixture into a foil-covered pie plate.
3. Place the pie plate in the Dutch oven, cover, and place the oven over the coals or campfire (on a rack).
4. Cook 25 minutes, or until the eggs are set.
5. Just before serving, sprinkle the cheese over the quiche and let it melt.

Nutrition

Calories 192, total fat 15.3 g, Carb 3.2 g, Protein 11.3 g, sodium 186 mg

8. Australian Damper

Preparation time: 20 minutes

Cooking time: 10 minutes

Servings: 5

Ingredients:

- 3 ½ cups self-rising flour
- 1 tablespoon lemon zest
- Salt, to taste
- ¾ cup almond milk, unsweetened
- 2 teaspoons sugar
- ¼ cup butter
- Pinch cinnamon

Directions

1. At home, combine all the listed ingredients to make a soft dough, and place it in a large plastic container.
2. To bake the bread, take out the dough from the container and knead it on a clean, floured, flat surface until smooth. Shape it into a round loaf.
3. Preheat a Dutch oven over the coals.
4. Grease a sheet of aluminum foil with oil and dust it with flour.

5. Place the loaf on the foil, and carefully place it in the Dutch oven.

6. Cover, and arrange a few coals on top. Let it cook for about 35 minutes until it sounds hollow when you tap on the bottom.

Nutrition

Calories 424, total fat 16.5 g, Carb 60 g, Protein 8.6 g, sodium 91 mg

9. Country Breakfast

Preparation time: 20 minutes

Cooking time: 45 minutes

Servings: 5

Ingredients:

- 1 pound pork sausage
- 2 cups frozen hash browns
- 12 eggs
- 2 cups cheddar cheese, shredded
- 1 container prepared biscuit dough

Directions

1. Place the Dutch oven over hot coals and cook the sausages in it until the meat is golden brown. Drain most of the fat.

2. Spoon or shake the prepared hash browns over the sausage.

3. Crack about 12 eggs over the hash browns, and sprinkle on the cheddar cheese.

4. Arrange the biscuits over the cheese.

5. Cover the Dutch oven, and place hot coals on the lid.

6. Cook for 45 minutes or until the eggs are set.

Nutrition: Calories 446, total fat 29.1 g, Carb 19.4 g, Protein 25.7 g, sodium 36 mg

10.   Breakfast Omelet

Preparation time: 20 minutes

Cooking time: 30 minutes

Servings: 5

Ingredients:

- 1 tablespoon butter
- 4 slices turkey bacon, chopped
- 8 eggs, beaten
- 1 cup cherry tomatoes, halved
- 1 cup baby spinach, chopped

Directions

1. Place a frying pan on a rack over hot coals, and melt the butter in it.

2. Add the turkey bacon and cook for 5 minutes, or until crisp.

3. Pour the eggs into the pan, and add the tomatoes and spinach.

4. When the eggs begin to set, gently left the omelet's edge and allowed the liquid egg to flow under the cooked layer. Repeat until the omelet is set. Do not stir.

Nutrition

Calories 316, total fat, 24 g, Carb 10 g, Protein 18.2 g, sodium 410 mg

11.   Crab & Fennel Spaghetti

Preparation time: 10 minutes

Cooking time: 50 minutes

Servings: 4

Ingredients:

- 160 g of mixed brown and white crabmeat from sustainable sources
- 1 fresh red chili
- 1 Fennel bulb
- 150 g of dried spaghetti
- 160 g of mixed cherry tomatoes

Directions:

1. Place the Dutch oven on medium-low heat. Trim the fennel, pick any leafy tops and reserve them, then halve the bulb and slice it finely. Put a tbsp of butter in the oven and cook for 5 minutes with the lid on.

2. Meanwhile, cook the pasta in the Dutch oven of boiling salted water according to the packet instructions, then drain and reserve a mug of the cooking liquid.

3. Slice the chili thinly, stir in the dutch oven and cook uncovered until soft and moist, occasionally stirring.

4. Cut the tomatoes into the oven for 2 minutes, followed by the crab meat, and drained pasta 1 minute later.

Season with sea salt and black pepper, sprinkle with one tablespoon of extra virgin butter, and sprinkle over any reserved fennel tops, if possible, with a reserved cooking water splash. Enjoy!

Nutrition

Calories 234, total fat 14.5 g, Carb 60 g, Protein 8.6 g, sodium 91 mg

12.   Epic Rib-Eye Steak

Preparation time: 10 minutes

Cooking time: 30 minutes

Servings: 4

Ingredients:

- 350 g mixed mushrooms
- Four sprigs of fresh rosemary
- 1 600 g jar of quality white beans
- 600 g, (ideally 5cm thick) piece of rib-eye steak, fat removed
- Four cloves of garlic

Directions

1. Place your Dutch oven on medium-high heat.

2. Rub the steak with a pinch of sea salt and black pepper all over, then sear on all sides for a minimum of 10 minutes, so you get the right color on the outside and keep it medium rare in the center, or cook to your liking, occasionally turning with tongs.

3. In the meantime, strip off the rosemary leaves' sprigs, cut and finely slice the garlic, and tear any more giant mushrooms. Transfer to a plate when the steak is finished and cover with tin foil.

4. Reduce heat to medium under the Dutch oven and crisp the rosemary for 30 seconds, then add garlic and mushrooms, then you cook for 8 minutes or always toss until golden.

5. Add 1 tbsp. of red wine vinegar and cook for 5 minutes, then season to perfection.

36

6. Pour over any remaining juices. Slice and serve with a little extra virgin butter at the table, if you like.

Nutrition: Calories 124, total fat 16.5 g, Carb 60 g, Protein 8.6 g, sodium 91 mg

13. Quinoa, Everyday Dals, And Avocado

Preparation time: 10 minutes

Cooking time: 35 minutes

Servings: 4

Ingredients:

- 1 Bag Maya Kaimal Everyday Dals of your choosing

- Half cup of quinoa (if you want more quinoa, then double the amount of rice and the amount of water)

- 1 avocado

- 1 cup of water

Directions:

1. You're going to use the same pot to heat the Dals and cook the quinoa.

2. Cook the quinoa first. Add the quinoa to the dish, cover with 1 cup of water and a little salt, then bring to a boil. Cover your pot once it has boiled and reduced it to medium-low heat and simmer until the water is

absorbed into the quinoa for about 15-20 minutes. Then pass the quinoa to your bowls for cooking.

3. While your oven is still warm, add the Everyday Dals and heat them for about 5 minutes (until they are cooked through), then serve on top of your quinoa.

4. Top with some avocado and enjoy.

Nutrition

Calories 124, total fat 11.5 g, Carb 60 g, Protein 8.6 g, sodium 91 mg

14.   Spiced Scones

PreparationTime: 15 minutes

CookingTime: 10 minutes

Servings: 6

Ingredients

- 2 cups self-rising flour
- 1 teaspoon cumin
- ⅛ teaspoon red pepper flakes, or to taste
- ¼ teaspoon salt
- 2 tablespoons butter
- ¾ cup milk

Directions

1. In a bowl, combine flour, cumin, chili, and salt.

2. Rub in butter until coarse-textured.

3. Add milk and mix.

4. Press out on a floured surface to make a ¾-inch thick round.

5. Cut into 6 wedges.

6. Cook in a nonstick frying pan or well-seasoned skillet over medium heat until browned and cooked through (about 5 minutes on each side).

Nutrition

Calories 186, Carbs 31.4 g, Fat 4.8 g, Protein 1.7 g, Sodium 670 mg

15.   Breakfast Scramble

Preparation Time: 5 minutes

Cooking Time: 15 minutes

Servings: 2

Ingredients

- 4 small red potatoes, diced
- ¼ cup water
- 1 tablespoon olive oil
- Pinch of salt
- 4 large eggs, beaten
- 1 tablespoon milk
- 1 scallion, thinly sliced
- ⅓ cup grated cheese
- 1 tablespoon fresh thyme or herb of choice, chopped

Directions

1. Combine potatoes, water, oil, and salt in a nonstick frying pan or well-seasoned skillet.

2. Cover and cook over high heat until almost all the water has dried out and potatoes begin to sizzle in the oil (about 5 minutes).

3. Remove lid and flip potatoes, cooking until lightly browned (about 5 minutes).

4. Beat the eggs and milk in a bowl. Then pour over the potatoes.

5. Add sliced scallion and mix to scramble until set (about 3 minutes).

6. Remove from heat and sprinkle with cheese and herbs.

7. Let sit until cheese melts (about 1 minute) and serve.

Nutrition

Calories 342, Carbs 15.5 g, Fat 22.7 g, Protein 19.3 g, Sodium 425 mg

16.   Breakfast Cinnamon Rolls

Preparation Time: 10 minutes

Cooking Time: 20–30 minutes

Servings: 6

Ingredients

- 2 (7½-ounce) packages of buttermilk biscuits
- ¼ cup butter, melted or softened to a spreadable consistency
- ¾ cup brown sugar, packed
- 1 teaspoon cinnamon
- ½ cup nuts or raisins (optional)

Frosting

- 1½ cups powdered sugar
- ¼ cup butter softened
- 1 teaspoon vanilla extract
- 2 tablespoons milk or a little more to get the right consistency

Directions

1. Heat coals until very hot for a 2- to 2¾- quart Dutch oven (about 8-inch diameter), set aside five coals for the bottom and 11 for the top.

2. Spray with nonstick spray, or rub the inside with a little oil.

3. Remove the biscuits from the packages and roll them out thinly.

4. Spread evenly with melted butter.

5. Sprinkle as evenly as possible with sugar, cinnamon, and nuts or raisins (if using).

6. Roll into rods. Note: These may be made in advance, wrapped in plastic, and frozen; allow them to thaw out during the trip.

7. Arrange in the Dutch oven, cutting as needed to make them fit.

8. Position over coals and place lid with coals on top.

9. Check about 18 minutes into cooking. Adjust the heat by removing or adding coals, as needed. Rotate the Dutch oven to ensure even heating.

10. Rolls should be done in 20–30 minutes. It should be fragrant and no longer doughy.

11. Remove from heat and let cool while you prepare the frosting (about 5 minutes).

12. Combine the sugar, butter, and vanilla. Gradually add the milk until the desired consistency is attained. It should be thick and pourable but not watery.

13. Drizzle over cooked rolls, or cut into pieces and drizzle with frosting individually.

Nutrition: Calories 656, Carbs 112.7 g, Fat 25.8g, Protein 5.7 g, Sodium 994 mg

17.   Eggs with Beans and Tomatoes

Preparation Time: 5 minutes

Cooking Time: 12–15 minutes

Servings: 2

Ingredients

- 2 tablespoons olive or canola oil
- 1 medium red onion, minced
- 2 teaspoons cumin
- ½ teaspoon red pepper flakes, or to taste
- Salt and pepper, to taste
- 1 (14-ounce) can diced tomatoes
- ½ (15-ounce) can cannellini beans
- 4 eggs

Fresh herbs of choice (like rosemary, basil, or sage), chopped

Directions

1. Heat oil in a nonstick pan or cast-iron skillet over medium heat.

2. Add onion and spices and sauté until fragrant (about 1 minute).

3. Season with salt and pepper and add tomatoes and beans.

4. Continue cooking, with occasional stirring, until onion is tender (about 5 minutes). Make four depressions in the mixture and crack an egg into each.

5. Cover and let cook until eggs are desired doneness (about 2–5 minutes).

6. Season again, as needed, and sprinkle with herbs.

7. Serve while hot.

Nutrition

Calories 354 Carbs 21.1 g Fat 23.2 g Protein 17.9 g Sodium 1028 mg

18.   Basic Hobo Pie

Preparation Time: 5 minutes

Cooking Time: 1–3 minutes

Servings: 5–6

Ingredients

1 loaf bread, sliced thickly into squares

¼ cup pizza sauce

Mozzarella cheese, sliced thinly or shredded

10–15 slices pepperoni, chopped

¼ cup butter, softened, or nonstick cooking spray

Directions

1. To prevent sticking, butter the bread slices that will be on the outer sides of the sandwiches, or simply spray the inside of the hobo pie maker with nonstick cooking spray.

2. Lay a slice, buttered side down (if not using nonstick spray) on the hobo pie maker.

3. Layer with pizza sauce (be sparing, as too much will spill out and burn), cheese, and pepperoni.

4. Top with the second slice of bread, buttered side up (if using butter).

5. Wrap in aluminum foil, if desired, for easier cleanup.

6. Close pie maker and place over coals, turning now and then until bread is toasted (about 1–3 minutes; heat from campfires varies a lot).

Other suggested Hobo Pie variations:

- Chocolate and marshmallows (s'mores)
- blueberry pie filling and butter or cream cheese
- ham and cheese
- peach pie filling and marshmallow
- peanut butter, marshmallow, and chocolate (rocky road)
- Nutella and strawberries
- sausage, egg, and cheese
- tuna and cheese
- use biscuit dough instead of bread

Nutrition (per serving)

Calories 220 Carbs 25.7 g Fat 8.8 g Protein 9.1 g Sodium 558 mg

19. Grilled Roast Beef Paninis

Preparation Time: 5 minutes

Cooking Time: 2 minutes

Servings: 1–2

Ingredients

- 2 slices of Italian bread (like ciabatta or Michetti)
- 1 tablespoon aioli garlic mustard
- 2 slices roast beef
- 2 slices provolone cheese
- ½ green pepper, grilled (optional)
- 2 tablespoons butter

Directions

1. Spread aioli over one side of each bread slice.
2. Place roast beef, cheese, and green pepper (if using) over one slice.
3. Place remaining bread slice on top.
4. Butter the outside of the bread slices.
5. Wrap in foil and place on grill or in hobo pie maker.
6. Grill until done (about 1–3 minutes, depending on heat from the campfire).

Nutrition (per serving)

Calories 349 Carbs 10.1 g Fat 24 g Protein 23.7 g Sodium 745 mg

20. Backcountry Breakfast

Preparation Time: 5–10 minutes

Cooking Time: 0 minutes

Servings: 2

Ingredients

- ¾ cup quick-cooking or instant oats
- ¼ cup powdered milk
- ⅓ cup raisins or dried apple bits
- ⅓ cup unsalted mixed nuts, chopped
- 2 teaspoons unsalted shelled sunflower seeds (optional)
- 1½ tablespoons brown sugar
- ½ teaspoon cinnamon
- 2 cups boiling water

Directions

1. Prepare in advance: Combine ingredients except for the boiling water in a Ziploc bag, shaking to mix. Set aside until ready for use.

2. To serve, place the mixture in a bowl and add boiling water. Let sit for 2 minutes. Mix and serve.

Nutrition (per serving)

Calories 343 Carbs 54.2 g Fat 14.4 g Protein 8.5 g Sodium 93 mg

21. Dutch Oven Pizza

Preparation Time: 20 minutes

Cooking Time: 15 minutes

Servings: 12 (yield: 2 pizzas

Ingredients

- Canola oil, for greasing, or nonstick cooking spray
- 1 tube pre-made pizza crust, divided
- 1 cup tomato or pizza sauce, divided
- 3 cups mozzarella cheese, shredded, divided
- ½ cup cheddar cheese, grated, divided
- Dash of garlic powder
- Salt and pepper, to taste
- 1 medium onion, sliced, divided
- 12 ounces pepperoni slices, divided

Directions

1. Heat up coals in a fire pit, shifting them to heat evenly.

2. Grease a Dutch oven.

3. Roll out the tube of dough and divide into 2.

4. Spread one piece over the bottom of the Dutch oven, pressing and patching if needed. Note: If you want two pizzas but only have one Dutch oven, line with aluminum foil or an aluminum pie pan so that you can easily remove the first when cooked and then add the second one.

5. Spread half of the sauce over the dough.

6. Season with garlic powder, salt, and pepper.

7. Arrange half of pepperoni and half of onion on top.

8. Place over hot coals.

9. Place lid and add about 8 coals on top.

10. Cook until crust is lightly browned and no longer doughy (about 10 minutes). Meanwhile, prepare the second pizza on a sheet of foil or in an aluminum foil pie pan using the remaining ingredients (remember to leave out the cheese for now).

11. Sprinkle the first pizza with the cheese and replace the lid. Add a few more pieces of coal to melt the cheese faster.

12. Remove from coals, let cool slightly, and remove pizza from the Dutch oven.

13. Carefully place the second pizza into the Dutch oven and bake as above.

Nutrition (per serving)

Calories 329 Carbs 20.3 g Fat 21.9 g Protein 17.3 g Sodium 1106 mg

22.   Simple Pizza Turnovers

Preparation Time: 5 minutes

Cooking Time: 15 minutes

Servings: 8

Ingredients

8–16 slices pepperoni, diced

¼ cup shredded mozzarella cheese

3–4 tablespoons pizza or tomato sauce, or as needed

1 tube flaky biscuit dough (to make 8 biscuits)

2 tablespoons butter (optional)

Directions

1. In a bowl, mix pepperoni and mozzarella.

2. Add pizza sauce gradually until pepperoni and cheese begin to stick together.

3. Flatten a biscuit and place a small amount in the middle. Do the same for the rest of the biscuits, distributing the filling as equally as possible.

4. Fold over and press edges together to seal.

5. Arrange on a nonstick pan or skillet and place over medium heat.

6. Melt butter in the pan and swirl to spread if using.

7. When the bottom is lightly browned, flip over to brown the other side (about 10–12 minutes total).

Nutrition

Calories 221 Carbs 25.1 g Fat 11 g Protein 5.6 g Sodium 774 mg

Chapter Three: Poultry

23.   Classic Chicken "Stir Fry"

Preparation time: 20 minutes

Cooking time: 10 minutes

Servings: 5

Ingredients:

- 4 cups cooked chicken, chopped
- 2 cups rice, cooked
- 1 green bell pepper, sliced
- 1 cup broccoli florets, chopped
- Cooking spray

Directions

1. In a large bowl, combine the chicken, rice, green pepper, broccoli. Mix well.

2. Create five double-layer rectangles of foil, and coat them with oil or cooking spray.

3. Divide the chicken mixture among the pieces of foil. Fold up the sides and create packets. Seal well.

4. Place the packets over warm coals for about 15 minutes.

Nutrition

Calories 514, total fat 5.1 g, Carb 66 g, Protein 46 g, Sodium 1207 mg

24.   Balsamic Vinegar Chicken

Preparation time: 30 minutes

Cooking time: 10 minutes

Servings: 5

Ingredients:

- 4 boneless, skinless chicken breast halves
- ¾ cup balsamic vinegar
- ¼ teaspoon soy sauce
- ½ cup pesto
- ½ cup honey mustard sauce

Directions

1. Place the chicken, vinegar, soy sauce, salt, and pepper in a Ziploc® bag. Let it sit for a few minutes.

2. Heat the grill over medium, and cook the chicken until it is browned on both sides and cooked through.

3. Serve with pesto and honey mustard sauce.

Nutrition

Calories 432, total fat 25 g, Carb 3.4 g, Protein 45 g, sodium 375 mg

25.   Chicken Over the Coals

Preparation time: 20 minutes

Cooking time: 10 minutes

Servings: 5

Ingredients:

- 1 (4-pound) fryer chicken
- ½ cup lemon juice
- 2 tablespoons vegetable oil
- 2 teaspoons thyme
- 1 teaspoon rosemary

Directions

1. Preheat the grill over a hot bed of coals.
2. Cut the chicken into four servings.
3. Remove any skin.
4. Combine the lemon juice, oil, thyme, and rosemary in a bowl, and brush it over the chicken—season with salt and pepper.
5. Grill the chicken, cavity-side down, and turn after a few minutes.
6. Baste the chicken with the sauce repeatedly while cooking.

7. Once the chicken is golden brown and cooked through, remove it from the heat.

Nutrition

Calories 123, total fat 17.2 g, Carb 10.2 g, Protein 82 g, sodium 631 mg

26.   Chicken Kebabs

Preparation time: 50 minutes

Cooking time: 10 minutes

Servings: 5

Ingredients:

- 2 pounds boneless, skinless chicken breasts
- 6 ounces mushrooms, trimmed
- 2 unpeeled oranges, cut into 12 wedges
- ⅓ cup vegetable oil
- 1–2 teaspoons curry powder

Directions

1. Slice the chicken into long pieces. Thread the pieces on wooden skewers, alternating with mushroom and orange pieces.

2. Once finished, place the skewers in a shallow plastic dish.

3. Pour this mixture over the skewers, making sure they are well coated. Allow them to marinate for 30 minutes.

4. Grill the kebabs over medium coals, turning after 5 minutes.

5. When they are golden brown and cooked through, they are ready to serve.

Nutrition

Calories 231, total fat 13.5 g, carb 7.7g, Protein 45 g, sodium 132 mg

27.   Chicken and Potatoes

Preparation time: 15 minutes

Cooking time: 35 minutes

Servings: 5

Ingredients:

- 5 large chicken breasts
- 5 small potatoes, cut into ½-inch slices
- 1 red onion, chopped
- 1 cup prepared barbecue sauce
- 1 teaspoon sesame seeds

Directions

1. Place the cast-iron Dutch oven on hot coals.
2. Shift the coals around the oven.
3. Add the chicken, potatoes, onions, and barbecue sauce, and stir.
4. Cover the oven with the lid and place 12 hot coals on the top. Let it cook for 35 minutes.
5. Once done, serve with a sprinkle of sesame seeds on top.

Nutrition

Calories 181 total fat 11, Carb 47 g, Protein 24.6 g, sodium 752 mg

28.   Creamy Santa Fe Chicken

Preparation Time: 5 minutes

Cooking Time: 30 minutes

Servings: 4

Ingredients:

- 1 pound chicken tenders
- 1 tablespoon butter
- 2 cup fresh corn kernels
- 2 cups salsa verde (fresh or jarred)
- 1 cup sour cream

Directions

1. Preheat oven to 350°F/177°C.
2. Add the butter to a skillet and heat over medium.
3. Add the chicken tenders and brown for 1-2 minutes per side. Add the corn kernels and cook for an additional 2 minutes.
4. Transfer the chicken and corn to a 9"x9" baking dish.
5. Pour the salsa verde over the chicken and bake for approximately 30 minutes. Remove from the oven and stir in the sour cream.
6. Serve immediately over rice or in tortilla shells, if desired.

Nutrition: Calories 128, total fat 13.2 g, carb 77 g, Protein 8.1 g, sodium 896 mg

29.   Mediterranean Chicken

Preparation time: 5 minutes

Cooking time: 30 minutes

Servings: 4

Ingredients:

- 4 boneless, skinless chicken breasts
- 1 tablespoon butter
- 2 cups cherry tomatoes, quartered
- 1 cup fresh mint leaves, torn
- 1 lemon, juiced, and zested

Directions

1. Season the chicken breasts with salt and pepper.
2. Heat the butter in a sauté pan over medium-high heat. Cook until browned on each side, approximately 5-7 minutes per side, depending upon thickness.
3. Add the tomatoes, mint leaves, lemon juice, and one teaspoon of the lemon zest. Reduce heat to medium and cook, stirring gently, until tomatoes begin to soften. Some of their natural juices are released, approximately 5 minutes.
4. Remove from heat and season with additional salt and pepper, if desired.

Nutrition: Calories 128, total fat 13.2 g, carb 77 g, Protein 8.1 g, sodium 896 mg

30.   Rosemary Chicken Bake

Preparation Time: 5 minutes

Cooking Time: 40 minutes

Servings: 4

Ingredients:

- 4 bone-in chicken breasts, skin removed
- 1 tablespoon butter
- 2 cups chicken stock
- 1 lemon, sliced
- 2 fresh rosemary sprigs

Directions

1. Preheat oven to 375°F/191°C

2. Add the butter to a skillet and heat over medium-high heat. Add the chicken to the skillet and cook until slightly browned, approximately 3-4 minutes per side.

3. Remove the chicken from the skillet and place it in a baking dish. Add ¼ cup of the chicken stock and one rosemary sprig to the chicken. Place in the oven and bake for 25-30 minutes, or until juices run clear.

4. Meanwhile, add the remaining chicken stock, rosemary, and lemon slices to the pan that the chicken was browned in. Turn heat to medium-high and bring to a gentle boil while stirring constantly. Boil for one minute before reducing heat to low. Simmer for ten minutes. Remove rosemary sprig and keep sauce warm over gentle heat.

5. Remove chicken from the oven and transfer to serving plates—spoon sauce, including lemon slices, over each chicken piece.

6. Serve immediately.

Nutrition:

Calories 428, total fat 13.2 g, carb 77 g, Protein 8.1 g, sodium 896 mg

31.   Chicken with Cornbread Stuffing

Preparation time: 5 minutes

Cooking time: 4 hours

Servings: 4

Ingredients:

- 4 boneless skinless chicken breasts
- 3 cups dried cornbread crumbs (prepackaged or fresh)
- 2 cups chicken stock
- ½ cup celery, finely diced
- 1 teaspoon dried sage

Directions

1. Season the chicken with salt and pepper, then place in a layer among the bottom of a crock pot.

2. In a bowl combine the cornbread crumbs, celery, and sage. Add additional salt and pepper, if desired.

3. Add the cornbread mixture over the top of the chicken.

4. Pour the chicken stock over the cornbread mixture, stirring if necessary to make sure corn bread is saturated.

5. Cover crock pot and heat on high for 4-6 hours, or until chicken juices run clear.

Nutrition: Calories 138, total fat 23.2 g, carb 77 g, Protein 8.1 g, sodium 896 mg

32.　Leek and Dijon Chicken

Preparation time: 15 minutes

Cooking time: 30 minutes

Servings: 4

Ingredients:

- 4 boneless skinless chicken breasts
- 1 tablespoon butter
- 1 cup leeks, sliced
- 1 tablespoon Dijon mustard
- 1 tablespoon water

Directions

1. Preheat oven to 200°F/93°C.

2. Add the butter to a large skillet and heat over medium heat. Add the chicken and brown evenly on all sides, approximately 7 minutes per side, depending upon thickness, until juices run clear.

3. Remove chicken from pan and place on an oven safe dish. Place in the oven to keep warm.

4. Add the leeks to the skillet that the chicken was cooked in and sauté over medium heat, stirring and scraping up any chicken residue that remained in the pan. Cook until soft and translucent, approximately 3-5 minutes.

5. In a small bowl, combine the Dijon mustard, and water. Mix well before adding to the pan with the leeks. Warm gently.

6. Remove chicken from the oven and place on serving plates. Top with warm leek and Dijon sauce before serving.

Nutrition:

Calories 231, total fat 12.2 g, carb 17 g, Protein 8.1 g, sodium 896 mg

33.   Asian BBQ Chicken

Preparation time: 15 minutes

Cooking time: 15 minutes

Servings: 4

Ingredients:

- 1 pound boneless chicken breast, cut into tenders
- 2 tablespoons soy sauce
- 2 tablespoons honey
- 1 teaspoon sesame oil
- 1 tablespoon garlic chili paste

Directions

1. Begin by preparing and preheating the grill (either indoor or outdoor grill).

2. In a small bowl, combine the soy sauce, honey, sesame oil, and chili paste. Mix until well blended.

3. Take chicken tenders and gently slide them lengthwise onto metal or bamboo skewers.

4. Baste each skewer with the BBQ sauce.

5. Place skewers on a grill and cooks for approximately 10-15 minutes, turning once, until chicken juices run clear. Remove from heat and serve immediately.

34.   Chicken Piccata

Preparation time: 5 minutes

Cooking time: 25 minutes

Servings: 4

Ingredients:

- 4 boneless, skinless chicken breasts
- ¼ cup butter
- 1 cup dry white wine
- ¼ cup lemon juice
- 3 tablespoons capers
- 1 teaspoon salt
- 1 teaspoon pepper

Directions

1. Preheat oven to 200°F/93°C.

2. Begin by gently pounding the chicken breasts until they are approximately ¼-inch thick. Season with salt and pepper.

3. Over medium-high heat, add the butter to a large sauté pan. Add the chicken and brown evenly on both sides, approximately 5-7 minutes per side, until juices run clear.

4. Transfer chicken, leaving remaining butter in the sauté pan, an oven-safe dish, and place in the oven to keep warm.

5. Add the dry white wine to the pan and reduce over medium heat for approximately 10 minutes, scraping the bottom of the pan occasionally to loosen any bits remaining from the chicken.

6. Add the lemon juice and capers. Cook for another 2 minutes.

7. Remove the chicken from the oven and place back in the pan. Heat through, spooning the sauce over the chicken for 1-2 minutes.

8. Transfer to serving plates and serve immediately.

Nutrition:

Calories 228, total fat 33.2 g, carb 17 g, Protein 8.1 g, sodium 896 mg

35.   Sweet chicken surprise

Preparation time: 10 minutes

Cooking time: 40 minutes

Servings: 3

Ingredients:

- 2 x 200 g free-range chicken legs
- 1 bulb of garlic
- 250 g mixed-color seedless grapes
- 100 ml red vermouth
- Four sprigs of fresh tarragon

Directions:

1. Preheat the oven to 180ºC.

2. Put Dutch oven on high heat. Rub the chicken all over with a ½ t a tbsp. of butter, season with black pepper and salt with the skin side down in the Dutch oven.

3. Fry for few minutes until golden, then lightly squash the unpeeled garlic cloves with the heel of your hand and add. Pick in the grapes.

4. Turn the chicken skin side up, pour in the vermouth, transfer to the oven to roast for 40 minutes, or until the chicken is golden and tender. The sauce is sticky and reduced.

5. Add a little water to the pan and give it a gentle shimmy to pick up all the sticky bits. Pick over the tarragon, and dish up.

36.　　Thai red chicken soup

Preparation time: 10 minutes

Cooking time: 120 minutes

Servings: 3

Ingredients:

- 1 butternut squash (1.2kg)
- 100 g Thai red curry paste
- 1 x 1.6 kg whole free-range chicken
- 1 bunch of fresh coriander (30g)
- 1 x 400 milliliter tin of light coconut milk

Directions:

1. Sit in a big, deep pan with the chicken.

2. Carefully halve the length of the squash, then cut the seeds into 3 cm chunks.

3. Slice the stalks of coriander, add the squash, curry paste, and coconut milk to the Netherlands oven, and then pour 1 liter of water. Cover and cook for 1 hour and 20 minutes at medium heat.

4. Use tongs to remove a platter from the chicken. Sprinkle some fat on the chicken from the soup sheet, then sprinkle with half the leaves of coriander.

5. Serve at the table with 2 forks to split the meat. Crush some of the squash using a potato masher, giving a thicker texture to your soup.

6. Taste, season to perfection with black pepper and salt, then divide between six bowls and sprinkle with the remaining coriander.

7. Add chicken and Shred, as you dig in.

Nutrition:

Calories 118, total fat 15.2 g, carb 37 g, Protein 8.1 g, sodium 896 mg

37.   Chicken in a Pot

Preparation time: 10 minutes

Cooking time: 5 hours

Servings: 3

Ingredients:

- 3-4 lb. whole frying chicken
- 1 tsp. poultry seasoning
- 1/4 tsp. basil

Directions:

1. Wash chicken and pat dry. Sprinkle cavity with poultry seasoning. Put in the Dutch oven and sprinkle with basil. Cover and bake for about 5 hours or until tender.

38.   Easy Chicken Dinner

Preparation time: 10 minutes

Cooking time: 30 minutes

Servings: 3

Ingredients:

- 2 Chickens
- Carrots
- Seasonings
- Flour
- Potatoes

Directions:

1. Cut vegetables and potatoes for eating into small pieces. Split eight pieces of the chicken. Chicken of the back. In a plastic bag, mix the flour and seasonings. Put two pieces of chicken in the bag at a time and shake.

2. Once coated, remove the chicken from the bag and repeat until all the chicken has been eaten. Place and shake the potatoes in the bag. Cut from the bag the vegetables.

3. In the Dutch oven, add around 1/2 inches of oil and put on the coals. Add chicken and brown on all sides when the oil is hot. Drain excess oil from the pot and remove the chicken from the dish. Return the chicken to the bowl.

4. Apply around 1/4 inch warm water. Place over chicken potatoes and vegetables. Cover the pot and place it on the coals.

5. Set on top of the oven, ten coals. Cook until chicken is tender for 1 hour. Check regularly to ensure that a small amount of moisture is always present in the Netherlands oven.

Nutrition:

Calories 128, total fat 14.2 g, carb 47 g, Protein 18.1 g, sodium 596 mg

39.   Easy Chicken Casserole

Preparation time: 10 minutes

Cooking time: 30 minutes

Servings: 3

Ingredients:

- 1 Whole chicken cooked, b1d, chopped
- 2 cans Cream of Chicken Soup or 1 can Golden Mushroom soup
- 1 c Mayonnaise
- 1 box "Stove Top" stuffing, chicken flavor
- Cheddar cheese

Directions:

1. Combine soup and mayonnaise in a massive bowl of choice. Then season pkg from stuffing mix and 3/4c stuffing crumbs.

2. Add chicken and mix well. Place in the Dutch oven, and then you top with remaining crumbs. Bake at 350 degrees Celsius for 30 min until bubbly and crumbs are brown. Variation change 1 can Golden Mushroom soup with Cream of Chicken soup. Add shredded cheddar cheese in the soup mixture, depending on your choice. You can sprinkle on it.

Nutrition:

Calories 318, total fat 23.2 g, carb 17 g, Protein 8.1 g, sodium 126 mg

40.   Scrambled egg omelet

Preparation time: 10 minutes

Cooking time: 30 minutes

Servings: 3

Ingredients:

- 350 g ripe mixed-color tomatoes
- ½-1 fresh red chili
- ½ a bunch of fresh basil (15g)
- Four large free-range eggs
- ½ x 125 g ball of moz.zarella

Directions:

1. Slice the tomatoes thinly, place them on a sharing tray, then dress with a little extra virgin butter, red vinegar, sea salt, and black pepper.

2. Put most of the basil leaves into a pestle and mortar, pound into a paste with a pinch of salt, then muddle extra virgin butter in 1 tablespoon to make basil oil.

3. Slice the chili finely. Cut the mozzarella perfectly.

4. Put the Dutch oven with half a tablespoon of butter on medium heat. Beat and pour in the eggs, stir periodically with a rubber spatula, gently pushing the eggs around the Netherlands oven.

5. Stop the stir and scatter the mozzarella at the center when they are gently scrambled but still loose, then drizzle over the basil oil.

6. Let the bottom of the rest of the egg for 1 minute, then use the spatula to flip it back to the center, then fold the top half back over as well. Turn it to the tomato platter upside down, right side up.

7. Slice down the center to reveal in the middle the oozy scrambled eggs

Nutrition:

Calories 128, total fat 15.2 g, carb 37 g, Protein 5.1 g, sodium 506 mg

Chapter Four: Vegetarian and Side Dish Recipes

41.   Grilled Sweet Potato Fries

Preparation time: 10 minutes

Cooking time: 20 minutes

Servings: 3

Ingredients:

- 2 Medium Sweet Potatoes

- 2 Tablespoons Butter or Vegetable Oil

- 1 Clove of Garlic, Chopped

- 1 Teaspoon Chili Powder

- 1 A packet of Ranch Dry Mix

Directions

1. Wash the Sweet Potatoes and dry them. Then cut them in lengthwise strips, about 1/3 an inch wide on each side, so they look like fries.

2. The important thing is that they must be uniform so they can cook up at the same time. If you wanted to produce crispier fries and have the time, soak the chips in water for about 30 minutes and then let them drain for an hour before continuing. If otherwise, then that's fine too; they'll still be delicious.

3. Mix all the recipe ingredients in a bowl. We want all the beautiful spices and dry mix to be uniformly covered.

Place the Dutch oven on a grate over an open fire or on the middle rack of a grill.

4. We're going to cook the potatoes and make them soft and crispy on the outside. You want about ten minutes per side, depending on your heat flipping once.

Nutrition:

Calories 110, total fat 10.2 g, carb 37 g, Protein 8.1 g, sodium 236 mg

42.   Blistered Shishito Peppers

Preparation time: 10 minutes

Cooking time: 20 minutes

Servings: 3

Ingredients

- 2 garlic cloves, sliced into chips
- 2 tablespoons oil
- 1 large shallot, thinly sliced

Directions:

1. Oil and garlic chips to a cold Dutch oven, and turn the heat on to medium. This will allow garlic to infuse the oil with flavor.

2. Observe the garlic chips, and remove them from the oil with a slotted spoon just when they begin to brown. It happens quickly, and they are easy to burn. Set aside.

3. Turn the heat up to medium-high, and add the peppers to the hot garlic oil. They will crackle and blister. Turn them occasionally until they are dried and blistered all over. You may have to remove smaller 1s before larger 1s.

4. Sprinkle the top with garlic chips, and either serve warm or pack in a jar for enjoying later.

Nutrition: Calories 128, total fat 12.2 g, carb 61 g, Protein 8.5 g, sodium 124 mg

43.   Bubble and Squeak

Preparation time: 10 minutes

Cooking time: 35 minutes

Servings: 3

Ingredients:

- 1 small head of cabbage or 1/2 large head, chopped
- Five medium potatoes, sliced in bite-size wheels
- 1 or 2 Polish or Kielbasa type sausages (all kinds I tried were great, even bulk sausage!)
- 1 cup of water
- Butter

Directions:

1. Get 1 pot (Dutch oven), layer chopped cabbage, potatoes, sausage, and then repeat until all ingredients are used.
2. Add water and Butter, cover, and simmer until cabbage and potatoes, and sausages are cooked. Probably about 15 or 20 minutes.

Nutrition:

Calories 134, total fat 10.2 g, carb 47 g, Protein 13 g, sodium 226 mg

44.   Sizzling seared scallops

Preparation time: 10 minutes

Cooking time: 20 minutes

Servings: 3

Ingredients:

- 200 g frozen peas
- 400 g potatoes
- ½ a bunch of fresh mint (15g)
- 6-8 raw king scallops (coral attached, trimmed, from sustainable sources)
- 50 g firm higher-welfare black pudding

Directions:

1. Wash the potatoes, chop into 3 cm chunks and cook for 1-2 minutes or until tender, adding the peas for the rest 3 minutes in the Dutch oven of boiling salted water.

2. Meanwhile, most of the mint leaves are picked and finely chopped and put aside.

3. Place 1 tablespoon of butter and leaves the remaining mint to crisp for 1 minute, then scoop the leaves onto a plate and leave the oil behind.

4. Season the scallops on each side for 2 minutes or until golden with sea salt and black pepper. Crumble it in the black pudding (so it chips next to each other).

5. Drain the potatoes and peas, return to the oven, properly mash with the chopped mint and 1 tablespoon of extra virgin butter, taste, and season.

6. Layer with the scallops and black pudding and sprinkle lightly with extra virgin butter.

Nutrition:

Calories 145, total fat 16 g, carb 35 g, Protein 8.1 g, sodium 812 mg

45.   Pan Toasted Couscous

Preparation time: 5 minutes

Cooking time: 30 minutes

Servings: 4

Ingredients:

- 2 cups chicken stock
- 1¼ cup couscous
- 1 tablespoon butter
- ¼ cup shallots, diced
- 1 lemon, juiced, and zested

Directions

1. Add the chicken stock to a saucepan and bring to a boil over medium-high heat.

2. Add the couscous and stir. Remove from heat, cover, and let sit 5-7 minutes, or until all liquid has been absorbed.

3. In a large sauté pan, heat the butter over medium heat. Add the shallots and cook for 2 minutes. Add 1 tablespoon of lemon juice and two teaspoons of lemon zest. Stir and cook for 1 minute.

4. Add the couscous into the sauté pan and increase the heat to high. Cook, often stirring for 10 minutes. Reduce the heat to medium-low and cook, occasionally stirring for 20 minutes.

5. Remove from heat and serve immediately.

Nutrition: Calories 138, total fat 12.2 g, carb 52 g, Protein 10.1 g, sodium 124 mg

46.   Fresh Cucumber Salad

Preparation time: 5 minutes

Cooking time: 0 minutes

Servings: 4

Ingredients:

- 3 cups cucumber, cubed
- 1½ cups watermelon, cut into small cubes
- ½ cup red onion, sliced
- ½ cup fresh cilantro, chopped
- 2 teaspoons fresh lime juice

Directions

1. In a large bowl, combine the cucumber, watermelon, and red onion.
2. Season with cilantro, lime juice, salt, and pepper. Mix well.
3. Place in the refrigerator and chill for at least 2 hours.
4. Stir well before serving.

Nutrition:

Calories 214, total fat 14 g, carb 17 g, Protein 4.1 g, sodium 456mg

47.   Sweet Roasted Root Vegetables

Preparation time: 5 minutes

Cooking time: 30 minutes

Servings: 4

Ingredients:

- ¼ cup butter, melted
- 2 cups carrots, chopped
- 1 cup sweet potato, diced
- 1 cup rutabaga, diced
- ¼ cup wildflower honey

Directions

1. Preheat oven to 400°F/204°C.
2. In a bowl, combine the carrots, sweet potato, and rutabaga.
3. Drizzle the vegetables with melted butter and honey. Season with salt and pepper. Toss well to coat.
4. Spread the vegetables out on a baking sheet. Place in the oven and bake for 30-35 minutes, or until vegetables are tender and caramelized.

Nutrition:

Calories 138, total fat 12.2 g, carb 77 g, Protein 3 g, sodium 1122 mg

48.   Fennel Gratin

Preparation time: 10 minutes

Cooking time: 60 minutes

Servings: 4

Ingredients:

- 3 cups fennel, sliced
- ¾ cup vegetable stock
- ¼ cup butter
- 1 cup fine bread crumbs
- 1 cup fresh grated parmesan cheese
- 1 teaspoon salt
- 1 teaspoon pepper

Directions

1. Preheat oven to 375°F/191°C.

2. Place the fennel slices in a lightly oiled 8"x8" baking dish. Cover with chicken stock and 2 tablespoons of butter cubed. Season with salt and pepper.

3. Cover and place in the oven—Bake for 35 minutes.

4. Meanwhile, in a small saucepan, melt the remaining butter. Add in the breadcrumbs, parmesan cheese, and additional salt and pepper, if desired.

5. Removed gratin from the oven and top with bread crumb mixture.

6. Recover the dish and place back in the oven. Bake for an additional 30-35 minutes, or until the fennel is tender.

7. Let rest 5 minutes before serving.

Nutrition:

Calories 328, total fat 12 g, carb 30g, Protein 9 g, sodium 126 mg

49.   Buttered Corn and Poblano Soup

Preparation time: 5 minutes

Cooking time: 30 minutes

Servings: 4

Ingredients:

- 1 tablespoon butter
- 4 cups fresh corn kernels
- 2½ cups milk
- 1 cup Monterey Jack cheese, shredded

Directions

1. In a Dutch oven, melt the butter over medium heat. Add the corn kernels and cook while stirring for approximately 3-4 minutes, or until corn is slightly toasted.

2. Add the milk and bring the mixture to a boil over medium-high heat for two minutes. Season with salt and pepper.

3. Transfer one half of the soup to a blender and pulse until creamy and thick. Return to the Dutch oven and mix well.

4. Gently reheat soup over low heat.

5. Serve immediately topped with Monterey jack cheese.

Nutrition: Calories 248, total fat 19.2g, carb 10g, Protein 8.1 g, sodium 196 mg

50.   Pita Pizza Blanco

Preparation time: 10 minutes

Cooking time: 15 minutes

Servings: 4

Ingredients:

- 4 pieces of pita bread
- ¾ cup crème Fraiche
- 3 cloves garlic, crushed and minced
- ½ cup fresh oregano, chopped
- 1½ cup fresh mozzarella cheese, sliced

Directions

1. Preheat oven to 420°F/216°C.

2. Spread out the pita bread pieces on one or two baking sheets.

3. In a bowl, combine the crème fraiche, garlic, and oregano. Blend well.

4. Spread the mixture evenly on each of the pita breads. Top with several slices of fresh mozzarella cheese.

5. Place in the oven and bake for 15 minutes, or until cheese is golden and bubbly.

6. Serve warm.

Nutrition: Calories 198, total fat 23.2 g, carb 37 g, Protein 6.1 g, sodium 126 mg

51.   Ancient Grain Stuffed Peppers

Preparation time: 5 minutes

Cooking time: 35 minutes

Servings: 4

Ingredients:

- 4 large red bell peppers, tops removed and seeds scooped out
- 3 cups ancient grain blend, cooked
- 1 tablespoon butter
- 2 cups white mushrooms, sliced
- ½ cup fresh parsley, chopped

Directions

1. Preheat oven to 350°F/177°C.
2. In a large bowl combine the ancient grains, butter, mushrooms, and parsley. Season with salt and pepper as desired.
3. Stuff each pepper liberally with the mixture and replace the tops of the peppers.
4. Transfer the peppers to a baking dish and add 1 tablespoon of water to the dish's bottom.
5. Place in the oven and bake for 35-40 minutes, or until peppers are tender.
6. Serve immediately.

Nutrition: Calories 167, total fat 15 g, carb 73 g, Protein 13 g, sodium 436 mg

52.   Parmesan Risotto

Preparation time: 10 minutes

Cooking time: 35 minutes

Servings: 4

Ingredients:

- 1 large shallot, finely chopped
- 2 quarts low-sodium vegetable or chicken broth, at room temperature
- 2 cups Arborio, carnaroli, or vialone nano rice
- ½ cup dry white wine
- 1 cup Parmesan cheese, finely grated

Directions

1. Add the butter to the Dutch oven and melt it over medium-high heat.
2. Mix in the rice until mixed well with the butter. Stir-cook for about 2 minutes until lightly toasted and aromatic.
3. Mix in the wine and simmer for 3 minutes until the wine is almost completely reduced and nearly dry.
4. Pour in the broth ½ cup at a time, stirring with each addition.
5. Cook for 20–30 minutes until the mixture is thickened and the rice is al dente.

6. Add some more butter and cheese, if desired.

7. Serve warm.

Nutrition

Calories 165, Fat 11 g, carbs 66 g, Protein 20 g, sodium 120 mg

53.   All-Time Favorite Mac and Cheese

Preparation time: 5 minutes

Cooking time: 35 minutes

Servings: 4

Ingredients:

- 3 cups of water
- 3½ cups whole milk
- 1 pound elbow macaroni
- 4 ounces Velveeta, cubed
- 2 cups sharp cheddar, shredded

Directions

1. Add the water, milk, and pasta to the Dutch oven. Stir and heat over medium-high heat.

2. Reduce heat to medium-low and simmer, stirring occasionally, for 12–15 minutes until the mixture is thickened and the pasta is tender.

3. Mix in the Velveeta and cheese and simmer over low heat until melted.

4. Serve warm.

Nutrition

Calories 344, Fat 14 g, carbs 39 g, Protein 16 g, sodium 450 mg

54. Creamy Mushroom Pasta

Preparation time: 5 minutes

Cooking time: 15 minutes

Servings: 4

Ingredients:

- 2 tablespoons butter
- ¾ pound mixed mushrooms (shiitake, cremini, oyster, etc.), sliced
- 3 cloves garlic, minced
- 1-quart chicken, mushroom, or vegetable broth
- Grated Parmesan cheese

Directions

1. Add the oil to the Dutch oven and heat it over medium-high heat.
2. Add the mushrooms and stir cook for about 4 minutes until lightly browned.
3. Add the garlic, cream, pasta, and broth and stir-cook for a few seconds.
4. Bring to a boil, and then reduce heat to low and simmer for about 12 minutes, occasionally stirring, until the pasta is cooked well and the mixture is thickened.
5. Serve warm with thyme and grated Parmesan on top.

Nutrition *:* Calories 607, Fat 26 g, carbs 71 g, Protein 20 g, sodium 1050 mg

55.   Mascarpone Pumpkin Pasta

Preparation time: 5 minutes

Cooking time: 15 minutes

Servings: 4

Ingredients:

- 1 cup canned pumpkin puree
- 1-quart vegetable broth
- 1 cup of water
- ¾ pound dry penne pasta
- 2 teaspoons fresh rosemary leaves, finely chopped

Directions

1. Add the pumpkin puree, broth, water, and pasta to the Dutch oven and bring to a boil over medium-high heat.
2. Reduce heat to low and simmer for 10–12 minutes until most of the liquid evaporates, stirring occasionally.
3. Mix in the mascarpone, rosemary
4. Stir-cook for about 2 minutes until the pasta is cooked to your satisfaction.
5. Serve warm with grated Parmesan on top.

Nutrition

Calories 245, Fat 4 g, carbs 43g, Protein 8 g, sodium 63 mg

56. Classic Cheesy Spaghetti

Preparation time: 10 minutes

Cooking time: 12 minutes

Servings: 4

Ingredients:

- ½ cup of water
- 1-quart chicken broth
- ¾ pound dry spaghetti
- 1 Parmesan cheese rind (optional)
- ¾ cup Pecorino-Romano cheese, grated

Directions

1. Add the water, broth, and pasta and Parmesan rind to the Dutch oven and bring to a boil over medium-high heat.

2. Simmer for 8–9 minutes until most of the liquid evaporates, stirring occasionally.

3. Mix in the Pecorino-Romano

4. Stir-cook for 2 minutes until the pasta is cooked to your satisfaction.

5. Remove the Parmesan rind.

6. Serve warm.

Nutrition: Calories 497, Fat 10.5 g, carbs 73.5 g, Protein 25 g, sodium 685 mg

57.   Braised Leeks

Preparation time: 15 minutes

Cooking time: 50 minutes

Servings: 4

Ingredients:

- 6 medium leeks (white portion and light green parts only), halved lengthwise
- ¼ cup butter
- 1 teaspoon dry rosemary (or 2 teaspoons fresh rosemary)
- 2 teaspoons sugar
- ½ cup dry white wine

Directions

1. Preheat the oven 350ºF (180°C).
2. Clean the leeks under cold running water to remove any remaining dirt.
3. Add the butter in the Dutch oven, and let melt over medium-low heat. Add the leeks and brown them on the cut side down for 2-3 minutes over medium heat.
4. Turn the leeks over, add the remaining ingredients. Stir to combine. Cover and place in the oven. Bake for 35-45 minutes checking midway to turn over the leeks back cut side down. Add a bit of water if needed to prevent the leeks from sticking to the bottom.

5. Remove from the oven once the leeks are tender. If there is lots of cooking juice, you can reduce it on the stove, uncovered, over medium-high heat until most of the liquid has evaporated.

Nutrition

Calories 153, Fat 5 g, carbs 18 g, Protein 3 g, sodium 77 mg

58.   French Onion Pasta

Preparation time: 10 minutes

Cooking time: 35 minutes

Servings: 4

Ingredients:

- 3 tablespoons butter
- 1½ pounds yellow onions, sliced paper-thin
- ⅔ Cup water
- 1-quart low-sodium vegetable or beef broth
- ¾ pound dry orecchiette pasta
- ⅓ cup ruby port
- 2 ounces (about ¾ cup) Gruyere cheese, finely shredded
- Salt and pepper to taste

Directions

1. Add the oil to the Dutch oven and heat it over medium-high heat.

2. Add the onion slices and stir-cook for 15–20 minutes until caramelized and dark.

3. Add the water, broth, pasta, and ruby port; stir and cook for 12 minutes until the liquid is evaporated.

4. Mix in the Gruyere. Season to taste with salt and pepper.

5. Serve warm.

Nutrition

Calories 520, Fat 12 g, carbs 84 g, Protein 17.5 g, sodium 1259 mg

59.   Seasoned French Fries

Preparation time: 5 minutes

Cooking time: 60 minutes

Servings: 4

Ingredients:

- 3 pounds russet potatoes, cut into ½-inch sticks
- 3 quarts peanut oil
- 2 teaspoons Old Bay seasoning

Directions

1. Add the potato sticks to a bowl and cover with cold water; set aside for 30–60 minutes. Drain and pat dry.
2. Add the peanut oil to the Dutch oven and heat it to 325°F (160°C).
3. In 2–3 batches, fry the potato sticks for 7–9 minutes until golden brown.
4. Drain over paper towels.
5. Increase heat to 400°F (200°C).
6. Return the cooked potato sticks to the Dutch oven in 2–3 batches and fry for 1–2 minutes until deep golden brown.
7. Drain over paper towels.
8. Serve warm.

Nutrition: Calories 226, Fat 7 g, carbs 39 g, Protein 5 g, sodium 397 mg

60.   Buttery Carrots

Preparation time: 10 minutes

Cooking time: 10 minutes

Servings: 4

Ingredients:

- 1 cup of water
- 2 pounds carrots cut into 2-inch pieces
- ⅓ Cup butter
- 2 tablespoons all-purpose flour
- 2 teaspoons chicken bouillon granules

Directions

1. Pour 1 inch of water into the Dutch oven.
2. Add the carrots and boil for 6–8 minutes until tender. Drain and set aside.
3. Add the butter and melt it over medium-high heat.
4. Add the onion and stir-cook until softened and translucent.
5. Add the flour and bouillon
6. Bring to a boil and then simmer for about 2 minutes until the mixture is thickened, stirring occasionally.
7. Stir in the carrots.

Nutrition: Calories 129, Fat 8 g, carbs 14 g, Protein 2 g, sodium 416 mg

61.   Baked Garlic and Mushroom Rice

Preparation time: 10 minutes

Cooking time: 40 minutes

Servings: 4

Ingredients:

- 3 tablespoons butter
- 1 pound mushrooms, diced
- 3 cloves garlic, minced
- 1½ cups of rice
- ½ cup white wine

Directions

1. Warm the butter in the Dutch oven over medium heat.
2. Stir in the diced mushrooms and minced garlic.
3. Cook for about 10 minutes and then stir in the rice.
4. Pour in the white wine and cook for 2 minutes. Pour in the water, bring to a boil, and cover.
5. Bake at 350°F (180°C) for about 25 minutes.
6. Remove the lid and cook uncovered for 5 minutes until the rice is set and nicely baked.

Nutrition

Calories 406, Fat 11.3 g, carbs 63.3 g, Protein 9 g, sodium 18 mg

62.   Quinoa with Mixed Vegetables and Artichoke Hearts

Preparation time: 5 minutes

Cooking time: 40 minutes

Servings: 4

Ingredients:

- 3 tablespoons butter
- 2 cloves garlic, minced
- 1 (14-ounce) bag of frozen vegetables
- ½ cup artichoke hearts, diced
- 2 cups quinoa, washed and rinsed

Directions

1. Warm the butter in the Dutch oven over medium heat.
2. Stir in the minced garlic, frozen veggies, and diced artichoke hearts.
3. Cook for 5 minutes and then stir in the quinoa.
4. Pour in the water and bring to a simmer.
5. Reduce heat to low, cover, and cook for 20 minutes.
6. Remove the lid and mix everything to fluff up the quinoa with the veggies.
7. Serve on plates.

Nutrition: Calories 490, Fat 15.9 g, carbs 72.8 g, Protein 15.9 g, sodium 67 mg

63.   Dutch Oven Vegetarian Lasagna

Preparation time: 5 minutes

Cooking time: 40 minutes

Servings: 4

Ingredients:

- 5 tablespoons butter
- 4 cups baby spinach
- ½ pound lasagna sheets
- 1 (28-ounce) can tomato sauce
- 4 cups grated mozzarella cheese

Directions

1. Warm the butter in the Dutch oven over medium heat.

2. Stir in the baby spinach

3. Cook for 5 minutes until the spinach wilts.

4. Stir in the tomato sauce and cook for 5 minutes.

5. Remove from heat and transfer all but a little of the filling to a bowl.

6. Add a layer of lasagna sheets to the Dutch oven. Add a layer of the filling and sprinkle with mozzarella cheese.

7. Repeat at least two more times or until you run out of lasagna sheets and filling. Sprinkle the top with mozzarella cheese and pepper.

8. Cover and bake at 350°F (180°C) for about 20 minutes.

9. Remove the lid and cook uncovered for about 15 more minutes until the mozzarella is golden brown.

10. Let cool slightly, then slice and serve.

Nutrition

Calories 490, Fat 24 g, carbs 54.6 g, Protein 19.3 g, sodium 1238 mg

64.   Cheesy Ravioli Pasta Bake

Preparation time: 5 minutes

Cooking time: 40 minutes

Servings: 4

Ingredients:

- 3 tablespoons butter
- 1 pound mushrooms, diced
- 4 (9-ounce) packages of spinach ravioli
- 1 (24-ounce) jar marinara sauce
- ½ pound mozzarella cheese, shredded

Directions

1. Warm the butter in the Dutch oven over medium heat. Add the diced mushrooms.
2. Stir in the marinara sauce.
3. Let the flavors marry together, and then add the ravioli.
4. Bring to simmer and transfer the Dutch oven to a preheated oven at 350°F (180°C).
5. Bake for 25–30 minutes.

Nutrition

Calories 747, Fat 37.4 g, carbs 69.3 g, Protein 36.1 g, sodium 2030 mg

65.   Vegetarian Jambalaya

Preparation time: 5 minutes

Cooking time: 35 minutes

Servings: 4

Ingredients:

- 2 tablespoons butter
- 1 (14-ounce) bag of frozen vegetables
- 2 (16-ounce) cans red beans, drained and rinsed
- 1 cup long-grain rice
- 1 (28-ounce) can diced tomatoes

Directions

1. Warm the butter in the Dutch oven over medium heat.
2. Stir in the frozen veggies and cook for 5–7 minutes.
3. Stir in the rice and cook for 2–3 minutes.
4. Stir in the diced tomatoes and water.
5. Mix and bring to a boil.
6. Reduce heat to low and simmer, covered, for 20 minutes.
7. Stir in the red beans and serve warm.

Nutrition

Calories 1113, Fat 9.9 g, carbs 202.2 g, Protein 59.4 g, sodium 489 mg

66.   Stuffed Zucchini

Preparation time: 20 minutes

Cooking time: 40 minutes

Servings: 5

Ingredients:

- 2 tablespoons butter
- 2 large onions, chopped
- 1 cup quinoa, rinsed
- 1 cup cannellini beans, drained
- ½ cup almonds, chopped

Directions

1. Place a cast-iron Dutch oven over the campfire or hot coals.
2. Heat the oil and sauté the onions.
3. Add the quinoa and water.
4. Bring the mixture to a boil, put on the lid, and let it cook for 10 minutes.
5. Transfer this cooked quinoa to a bowl, and add the beans and almonds.
6. Cut the zucchini lengthwise, and scoop out the seeds.
7. Fill the zucchinis with the quinoa stuffing.
8. Wipe out the Dutch oven with a paper towel, and spray it with cooking spray.

9. Arrange the zucchinis in the Dutch oven. Cover, and place it over the heat.

10. If you're using charcoal, then put some coals on the lid.

11. Cook it for about 25–30 minutes.

12. When the zucchinis are fork-tender, serve.

Nutrition

Calories 407, total fat 13.2 g, Carb 58 g, Protein 18.5 g, sodium 34 mg

Chapter Five: Meat Recipe

67.   Country Style Ribs

Preparation Time: 10 minutes plus 24 hours marinating time

Cooking Time: 35 minutes

Servings: 6

Ingredients

- 6 pounds country-style pork ribs
- Barbecue sauce, for basting
- Marinade
- 3 tablespoons olive oil
- ⅓ cup hoisin sauce
- ⅓ cup soy sauce
- 4 teaspoons minced ginger
- ¾ cup whisky
- Zest of one orange
- Juice of one orange
- ½ cup light brown sugar
- 6 cloves garlic, minced
- 2 cups barbeque sauce

Directions

1. Place ribs in a large pot or Dutch oven and cover with water. Bring to a boil and continue until partly cooked (about 20 minutes). Drain well.

2. Combine ingredients for the marinade.

3. Place ribs with the marinade in a shallow container with a lid or a large Ziploc bag.

4. Let marinate, refrigerated, for 24 hours to 2 days.

5. Bring to room temperature before grilling.

6. Grill over medium heat for about 15 minutes, flipping frequently and basting with barbecue sauce.

Nutrition

Calories 985 Carbs 23.5 g Fat 56 g Protein 94.1 g Sodium 1025 mg

68.   Camper's Beer Braised Short Ribs

Preparation Time: 10 minutes

Cooking Time: Slow Cooker: 8 hours; Dutch Oven: 2 hours

Servings: 3–4

Ingredients

- 3 pounds beef short ribs, bone-in
- 3 medium onions, cut into wedges
- 1 bay leaf

Sauce

- 1 (12-ounce) bottle beer
- 2 tablespoons brown sugar
- 2 tablespoons Dijon mustard
- 2 tablespoons tomato paste
- 2 teaspoons dried thyme
- 2 teaspoons beef bouillon granules
- 1 teaspoon salt
- ¼ teaspoon pepper

Slurry (optional)

- 3 tablespoons all-purpose flour
- ½ cup cold water

Directions

1. Slow Cooker: Place ribs, onions, and bay leaf in a slow cooker. Combine sauce ingredients and add to ribs. Cover and cook for 8 hours on Low. Transfer ribs and onions to

a bowl or wrap in foil and set aside. Heat the remaining juices in a saucepan over medium heat until reduced and thickened. If desired, mix slurry ingredients in a small bowl and stir into juices for a thicker sauce. Spoon over ribs and serve.

2. Dutch Oven: Arrange coals in a ring (about 7 briquettes) in the cooking pit, leaving a space at the center. Place ribs, onions, and bay leaf in the Dutch oven. Mix sauce ingredients together and pour over ribs. Cover and place briquettes (about 13) in a ring on the lid. Rotate lid every 30 minutes for even cooking and replace briquettes as needed. Cook until ribs can be pierced easily and flesh pulls away from the bone at the ends (internal temperature: 180–190°F). Transfer ribs and onions to a bowl or wrap in foil and set aside. Heat the remaining juices until reduced and thickened. If desired, mix slurry ingredients in a small bowl and stir into juices for a thicker sauce. Spoon over ribs and serve.

Nutrition

Calories 418 Carbs 22 g Fat 19 g Protein 46 g Sodium 821 mg

69.   Walking Tacos

Preparation Time: 10 minutes

Cooking Time: 10 minutes

Servings: 2–4

Ingredients

- 1 pound ground beef
- 1 packet taco seasoning mix
- 1 medium tomato, chopped
- ¼ head lettuce, shredded
- 1 small onion, chopped
- 1 cup shredded cheese of choice (like cheddar or Monterey)
- ½ cup sour cream
- ¼ cup taco sauce
- 2–4 individual bags of corn chips, opened neatly on top

Directions

1. Brown beef over medium heat in a nonstick pan or cast-iron skillet.
2. Add seasoning and cook according to package instructions.
3. Divide into 2–4, depending on the number of packets.
4. Add to packets of corn chips.
5. Add other ingredients as desired.
6. Stir with a fork and eat directly from the packets.

Nutrition: Calories 653 Carbs 23.4 g Fat 48.6 g Protein 31 g Sodium 558 mg

70.   Tinfoil Sausage & Veggies

Preparation Time: 15 minutes

Cooking Time: 10–20 minutes

Servings: 4–6

Ingredients

- 1 red bell pepper, seeded and sliced thinly
- 2 ears shucked corn, cut into 1-inch disks
- 1 medium onion, chopped
- 4–5 small red potatoes cut into bite-size pieces
- 1 medium-sized zucchini, sliced
- 1 (13-ounce) package smoked turkey sausage, sliced
- Parsley, chopped, for sprinkling

Seasoning

- 5 tablespoons olive oil
- 1 tablespoon dried oregano
- 1 tablespoon dried parsley flakes
- ½ teaspoon garlic powder
- 1 teaspoon paprika
- Salt and pepper, to taste

Directions

1. Mix seasoning ingredients together in a large bowl.

2. Add bell pepper, corn, onion, potatoes, zucchini, and sausage. Toss to coat with seasoning.

3. For one serving, stack two sheets of foil together or use one sheet of heavy-duty aluminum foil. Place about a fourth of the seasoned veggie-and-sausage mix at the center of the foil. Fold over and seal. Repeat with remaining ingredients.

4. Place on preheated grill and cook until veggies are crisp-tender (about 10–20 minutes).

5. Remove from heat and serve sprinkled with chopped parsley.

Nutrition: Calories 333 Carbs 31.2 g Fat 17.1 g Protein 16 g Sodium 398 mg \

71.   Foil Hamburgers

Preparation Time: 15 minutes

Cooking Time: 30–40 minutes

Servings: 4

Ingredients

8 small new potatoes, unpeeled, quartered

1 teaspoon seasoned salt, or to taste

1 teaspoon Italian seasoning, or to taste

4 (¼-pound) frozen hamburger patties

1 cup frozen cut green beans

1 tablespoon olive oil

Directions

1. Stack 2 aluminum foil sheets on top of each other (or use one sheet of heavy-duty foil). Place one patty, ¼ of potatoes, and ¼ of green beans on the center of the stacked sheets. Sprinkle with about ¼ teaspoon each seasoned salt, Italian seasoning (or to taste), and olive oil. Fold sides of the foil over, leaving room for steam, and seal securely. Repeat for remaining ingredients.

2. Place on preheated grill at medium heat and cover. Let cook until patties are done (internal temperature: 160°F) and vegetables are tender (about 30–40 minutes), flipping the packets over midway through cooking.

3. Open carefully to release steam and serve.

Nutrition: Calories 410 Carbs 41 g Fat 16 g Protein 25 g Sodium 420 mg

72. A meal in a Can

Preparation Time: 5 minutes

Cooking Time: 35–45 minutes

Servings: 1

Ingredients

- 1 (about ¼-pound) hamburger patty
- 1 small red potato, quartered
- ⅓ medium carrot, peeled and cut into chunks
- 1 tablespoon chopped onion
- ½ small Roma tomato
- 2 tablespoons corn kernels
- 1 tablespoon butter or olive oil
- Salt and pepper, to taste

Directions

1. Layer the ingredients as listed in a clean coffee can.

2. Cover tightly with foil. This may be kept in a cooler until the campfire or grill is ready.

3. Place on a grate over the campfire or coals at about medium heat.

4. Let cook until potatoes are done (about 35–45 minutes).

Nutrition

Calories 556 Carbs 36.1 g Fat 34.8 g Protein 23.3 g Sodium 571 mg

73.   Beef & Potato Packets

Preparation time: 30 minutes

Cooking time: 25 minutes

Servings: 5

Ingredients:

- 1 tablespoon butter
- 2 tablespoons sherry vinegar
- 1 medium sweet potato, peeled and thinly sliced
- ½ cup onion, sliced
- 4 (6 ounces) servings of beef steak, trimmed of fat

Directions

1. Combine the oil, sherry vinegar, sweet potato, and onion in a bowl. Let it sit for few minutes.

2. Layout four double-layer sheets of foil, and coat the foil with cooking spray.

3. Using a slotted spoon, remove the vegetables from the sauce, and arrange them on the four foil pieces.

4. Place the meat in the sauce, and turn it to coat.

5. Top each serving with a piece of steak, and pour the sauce over.

6. Seal the packets, and place them on the grill.

7. Cook for 25 minutes, turning halfway.

8. Check that the steak is cooked to your liking and serve.

Nutrition: Calories 566, total fat 41 g, Carb 12.7 g, Protein 34.2 g, sodium 165 mg

74.   Ann's Brisket

Preparation time: 10 minutes

Cooking time: 20 minutes

Servings: 3

Ingredients:

- 3-4 lb. beef brisket
- 2-3 tbsp.. flour
- Seas1d tenderizer

Directions

1. Tenderizer coat brisket well. Wrap with 2 heavy-duty foil covers. Chill overnight. Cover and cook 225 to 250 for about 7 hours in the Dutch oven. You can cook it more quickly, but it's slowly cooked juicier.

2. Remove the foil and put it on a warm serving plate. Create a thin gravy with milk, rice. Before serving, pour over the brisket.

Nutrition:

Calories 408, total fat 11.2 g, carb 12 g, Protein 12.1 g, sodium 806 mg

75.   Beef and Vegetable Stir Fry

Preparation time: 10 minutes

Cooking time: 35 minutes

Servings: 3

Ingredients:

- 1 tablespoon butter
- 1 (16-ounce) package frozen mixed vegetables
- 1 cup stir fry sauce
- 2 teaspoons cornstarch
- 2 cups cubed cooked roast beef

Directions:

1. Get your oven in the Netherlands, heat the oil. Remove the frozen vegetables and remove some water when the oil is hot, then stir—cover and cook for 3 minutes over medium heat.

2. In a small bowl, mix the stir fry sauce with the cornstarch. Pour the vegetables into the Netherlands oven and mix. Then add and stir the cooked beef.

3. Replace the cover, cook the beef and vegetables at low heat for 5 to 8 minutes, occasionally stirring, till the meat is tender, while the vegetables are still crisp.

Nutrition: Calories 178, total fat 14.2 g, carb 17 g, Protein 12.1 g, sodium 126 mg

76.   Balsamic Braised Beef Ribs

Preparation time: 10 minutes

Cooking time: 6 hours

Servings: 3

Ingredients:

- 3 pounds short ribs
- 7 cloves garlic, crushed
- 2 cups tomato sauce (fresh or canned)
- ¾ cup balsamic vinegar
- 1 cup fresh figs, chopped

Directions

1. Take crushed garlic cloves and rub briskly over the short ribs. Cut the ribs and place them, along with any remaining garlic pieces, into a slow cooker.

2. In a small bowl, combine the tomato sauce, balsamic vinegar, and figs. Pour over the ribs and toss to coat.

3. Cook over low heat for 6-8 hours until ribs are fall off the bone tender.

Nutrition:

Calories 178, total fat 23 g, carb 12 g, Protein 9.1 g, sodium 126 mg

77. Grandma's Weekend Roast

Preparation time: 10 minutes

Cooking time: 125 minutes

Servings: 3

Ingredients:

- 1 4-pound beef roast
- ¼ cup butter
- 3 cups yellow onion, sliced
- 3 cups beef stock
- 1 cup red wine

Directions

1. Preheat oven to 325°F/163°C

2. Heat the butter in a Dutch oven over medium to medium-high heat.

3. Add the roast to the Dutch oven and brown evenly, approximately 3-5 minutes, on each side.

4. Remove meat from pan and temporarily set aside.

5. Add the onions to the pan, and cook until slightly soft, approximately 5 minutes.

6. Stir in the beef stock and red wine, and cook while stirring for 5-7 minutes. Season with additional salt and pepper, if desired.

7. Add the roast back into the Dutch oven, cover, and place in the oven. Cook for 2 hours, turn roast and then cook an additional 45 minutes.

8. Let roast rest 10 minutes before serving. Serve dressed with tender onions and pan sauce.

Nutrition:

Calories 147, total fat 12.2 g, carb 47 g, Protein 5.1 g, sodium 106 mg

78.   Flank Steak Roulade

Preparation time: 10 minutes

Cooking time: 65 minutes

Servings: 3

Ingredients:

- 1 2-pound flank steak, trimmed
- 1 tablespoon butter
- 3 cups fresh spinach, chopped
- 2 cups tomatoes, chopped
- 2 tablespoons prepared horseradish

Directions

1. Preheat oven to 425°F/218°C

2. Heat the butter over medium heat in a sauté pan. Add the spinach and tomatoes. Cook until spinach is wilted and tomatoes have begun to release a good amount of juice, approximately 4-5 minutes. Remove from heat.

3. Add one tablespoon of the horseradish to the spinach mixture. Mix well and set aside. Using a mallet, pound steak until it is approximately ¼-inch thick.

4. Take any butter that remains in the sauté pan and drizzle over the steak. Season with the remaining horseradish, salt, and pepper. Rub the mixture into the steak before turning the meat over.

5. Spread the spinach mixture along the steak. Starting at one end, begin rolling the steak lengthwise to create a pinwheel. Secure the pinwheel with several pieces of chef's twine.Place the roll into a baking pan and bake for 45-50 minutes.

6. Let rest for 10 minutes before removing twine and slicing into pieces 1½-inch thick for serving.

Nutrition: Calories 343, total fat 12.2 g, carb 77 g, Protein 32.1 g, sodium 136 mg

79.   Jalapeño Beef Pouches

Preparation time: 10 minutes

Cooking time: 45 minutes

Servings: 3

Ingredients:

- 2 pounds thin beef steak
- ¼ cup fresh cilantro
- 1 lime, quartered
- 1 tablespoon butter

Directions

1. Preheat oven to 350°F/177°C

2. Take one 18"x18" or larger piece of aluminum foil and lay it on a baking sheet.

3. Drizzle the foil with butter.

4. Cut the steak into four sections. Place steaks in the center portion of the foil.

5. Place jalapeños over the steaks and top with fresh cilantro and lime wedges.

6. Fold over the foil, creating a snug but not overly tight pouch around the meat, taking care to make sure that it is well sealed to avoid any juices escaping during cooking.

7. Place in the oven and cook for 35-40 minutes, or until steak has reached desired doneness.

8. Let rest 5-10 minutes before serving.

Nutrition:

Calories 138, total fat 13.2 g, carb 77 g, Protein 8.1 g, sodium 126 mg

80. Steak and Crispy Beet Salad

Preparation time: 10 minutes

Cooking time: 45 minutes

Servings: 3

Ingredients:

- 1 pound beef steak
- 4 cups baby spinach, torn
- 2 cups beets, cut into small cubes
- ¼ cup shallots, sliced
- ¼ cup butter

Directions

1. Preheat oven to 400°F/204°C

2. Place the beet cubes on a baking sheet and drizzle with 2 tablespoons of the butter. Place in the oven and roast for 25-30 minutes, or until beets are caramelized and slightly crispy.

3. Add enough oil to a skillet to coat the bottom surface and heat over medium-high.

4. Season the steak liberally with salt and pepper. Pan sear the steak evenly on all sides for approximately 7 minutes for a one-inch steak. This time may vary depending upon the thickness and desired doneness.

5. Remove the steak from the heat and set it aside on a plate to rest.

6. Add the rest of the oil to the pan. Heat over medium.

7. Add the shallots to the pan and sauté until translucent, approximately 3-5 minutes.

8. Remove the beets from the oven and add them to the skillet. Toss while cooking for 3 minutes, or just long enough to crisp the beets' outsides just slightly.

9. Place the spinach in a serving bowl. Add the beets and shallots, along with a little of the butter and steak drippings, if desired. Toss gently.

10. Slice the steak and top the salad with the steak right before serving.

Nutrition:

Calories 321, total fat 13.2 g, carb 12 g, Protein 11 g, sodium 756 mg

81.   Ginger Spiced Beef

Preparation time: 10 minutes

Cooking time: 35 minutes

Servings: 3

Ingredients:

- 1 pound flank steak, sliced into ½-inch strips
- ½ cup cornstarch
- 1 tablespoon sesame oil
- ¼ cup fresh grated ginger
- 1 medium orange, juiced, and zested

Directions

1. Mix cornstarch and water in bowl. Whisk until smooth and free of any lumps.

2. Heat the sesame oil over medium in a large sauté pan. Add the ginger to the oil and cook for 1 minute, or until fragrant.

3. Dip each strip of steak into the cornstarch mixture and place into the pan. Cook while tossing gently for 5-7 minutes.

4. Add ¼ cup fresh orange juice and 1 tablespoon orange zest. Cook while stirring for an additional 3-5 minutes, or until steak is cooked through.

5. Remove from heat and serve with rice, if desired.

Nutrition: Calories 143, total fat 15 g, carb 13 g, Protein 12 g, sodium 256 m

Chapter Six: Soup and Stew

82.　　Camper's Onion Soup in Foil

Preparation Time: 5 minutes

Cooking Time: 40–60 minutes

Serving: 1

Ingredients

- 1 large onion
- 1 beef bouillon cube, crumbled
- 1–2 tablespoons softened or melted butter
- Dash of black pepper (optional)
- Grated Parmesan and/or Swiss cheese for sprinkling
- 1 slice baguette or any bread of choice, toasted

Directions

1. Butter one side of a thick sheet of aluminum (large enough to cover the whole onion, plus extra for twisting to seal and to serve as a 'tail' for easy handling).

2. Peel the onion and core like an apple, but not to the bottom; leave a 'well' at the center.

3. Fill the well with crumbled bouillon and butter.

4. Fold the aluminum over the onion and twist the ends to seal.

5. Place in coals, over the grill, or around campfire edges (find a place where heat is moderate and relatively even).

6. Cook until tender or easy to squeeze with tongs (about 40–60 minutes).

7. Place in a bowl and open the foil. Sprinkle with black pepper and cheese.

8. Serve with a baguette slice.

Nutrition

Calories 299 Carbs 25.9 g Fat 19.6 g Protein 6.1 gSodium 1152 mg

83. Easiest Beef Stew

Preparation Time: 2 minutes

Cooking Time: 10 minutes

Serving: 4

Ingredients

1 pound lean ground beef

1 (15-ounce) can of mixed vegetables

2 (11½-ounce) cans V–8 vegetable juice or tomato juice

Directions

1. Cook the ground beef in a Dutch oven in its juices until evenly browned (about 8–10 minutes).

2. Drain off any juices.

3. Add the rest of the ingredients.

4. Bring to a boil.

5. Reduce heat and let simmer until all the vegetables are heated through.

Nutrition

Calories 386 Carbs 16.8 g Fat 23.7 g Protein 23.8 g Sodium 537 mg

84.   Corn and Sweet Potato Chowder

Preparation Time: 10 minutes

Cooking Time: 20 minutes

Servings: 4

Ingredients

- 4 bacon strips, chopped
- 1 medium onion, diced
- 2 (11-ounce) cans whole kernel corn, liquid drained into a separate container
- 2 cups water
- 1 (14.75-ounce) can cream of corn
- 4 medium-sized sweet potatoes, peeled and diced
- Salt and pepper, to taste

Directions

1. Cook the bacon in a deep pot until crisp. Optional: Scoop or drain out rendered fat as desired, leaving just enough to sauté onion.

2. Add onion and sauté until transparent (about 3–5 minutes).

3. Pour in water and corn liquid.

4. Bring to a boil.

5. Add sweet potatoes and cook until tender (about 5 minutes).

6. Stir in kernels and cream of corn.

7. Cook until heated through.

8. Season with salt and pepper.

Nutrition (per serving)

Calories 158 Carbs 24.2 g Fat 3.3 g Protein 8.5 g Sodium 919 mg

85.   Stuffed Bell Peppers

Preparation time: 20 minutes

Cooking time: 30 minutes

Servings: 5

Ingredients:

- 6 large bell peppers, tops off, seeds removed
- 2 tablespoons vegetable oil
- 1 pound ground beef
- 2 cups white rice (cooked at home)
- ½ cups tomato sauce

Directions

1. Place the Dutch oven in the coals to heat.

2. Add the vegetable oil, beef, and cook until brown.

3. Add the tomato sauce and precooked rice, and mix well.

4. Spoon the filling into the cored bell peppers. Wipe out the oven with a paper towel.

5. Arrange the stuffed bell peppers in the Dutch oven, and cover. Place some coals on the lid.

6. Bake for 20 to 30 minutes until the peppers are tender.

7. Serve and enjoy.

Nutrition

Calories 480, total fat 10 g, Carb 66 g, Protein 30.5 g, sodium 306 mg

86.   Sausage, Pepper & Potato Packets

Preparation time: 20 minutes

Cooking time: 25 minutes

Servings: 5

Ingredients:

- 3 red potatoes, cut in chunks
- 4 cooked dinner sausages, sliced
- 2 onions, sliced
- 2 tablespoons butter
- ½ teaspoon paprika

Directions

1. Mix all the ingredients in a large bowl.

2. Cut a long piece of heavy-duty foil into a 12x20 inch rectangle, and coat it with cooking spray.

3. Place the mixture in the center of the foil and enclose it to form a package.

4. Cook the packet a few inches above the coals on a grill rack, turning it twice.

5. After 25 minutes, check that the potatoes are cooked through. Serve!

Nutrition

Calories 434, total fat 22.5 g, Carb 30.3 g, Protein 24 g, sodium 688 mg

87.   Chicken Mushroom Soup

Preparation time: 10 minutes

Cooking time: 25 minutes

Servings: 5

Ingredients:

- 2 celery ribs, chopped
- 1-quart chicken broth
- ⅓ cup all-purpose flour
- 2 cups cooked chicken, cubed
- 1 (8¾-ounce) package precooked chicken-flavored rice

Directions

1. Add the oil to the Dutch oven and heat it over medium-high heat.
2. Add the vegetables and stir-cook until the carrots become soft, crisp, and tender.
3. Add the broth and flour to a mixing bowl. Mix well.
4. Pour the broth into the Dutch oven and bring to a boil, stirring occasionally.
5. Stir-cook for 5–6 minutes until thickened.
6. Add the other ingredients and cook over medium-low heat until cooked to satisfaction.
7. Serve warm.

Nutrition: Calories 224, Fat 7 g, carbs 23 g, Protein 15 g, sodium 741 mg

88. Creme Potato Chicken Soup

Preparation time: 10 minutes

Cooking time: 10 minutes

Servings: 5

Ingredients:

- 3½ cups water
- 4 cups shredded cooked chicken breast
- 2 (10¾-ounce) cans condensed cream of chicken soup, undiluted
- 1 pound frozen mixed vegetables, thawed
- 1 (14½-ounce) can potatoes, drained and diced

Directions

1. Add the water, chicken breast, chicken soup, vegetables, and potatoes to the Dutch oven. Bring to a boil.

2. Reduce heat to low, cover, and simmer for 8–10 minutes until the veggies are tender, stirring occasionally.

3. Mix in the cheese.

4. Serve warm with minced chives on top.

Nutrition

Calories 429, Fat 22 g, carbs 23 g, Protein 33 g, sodium 1464 mg

Chapter Seven: Dessert Recipes

89.   Granola Over A Campfire

Preparation time: 10 minutes

Cooking time: 35 minutes

Servings: 4

Ingredients:

- ½ Cup Vegetable Oil
- 6 Cups Rolled Oats
- ½ to 1 Cup Maple Syrup
- 2 Cups Pecans or Almonds
- 1 cup Dried Cranberries

Directions:

1. Get your Dutch oven. Add your nuts and toss them around. It's a good idea to take the oven off the fire as you throw them around to ensure you do not burn them.

2. Once they begin to have a sweet smell of nutty, you can add the rolled oats. Cook this over the fire slowly until it transforms or becomes brown and nutty.

3. Take the oven off the heat and add the Vegetable oil and the Maple Syrup. You may add more or make it less syrup depending on the consistency you need.

4. Toss this together and put it in a bowl when it's ready. Add the dried Cranberries and eat warm. You can keep it covered also, and it will last for more Breakfasts to come.

Nutrition:

Calories 108, total fat 12.2 g, carb 37 g, Protein 8.1 g, sodium 146 mg

90.   Wildberry Mascarpone Sliders

Preparation time: 15 minutes

Cooking time: 30 minutes

Servings: 4

Ingredients:

- 1 sheet puff pastry dough
- 2 cups fresh berry mixture, chopped
- ½ cup sugar
- ½ cup fresh basil chopped
- ½ cup mascarpone cheese

Directions

1. Lay the puff pastry dough out onto a flat surface. Using a cookie cutter or small glass, cut out circles approximately 1½" to 2" in diameter. Place on a cookie sheet and bake according to package instructions. Remove from oven and let cool.

2. In a bowl, combine the berries and sugar.

3. In another bowl, combine the basil and mascarpone cheese.

4. Spread the mascarpone mixture onto each puff pastry round. Top with a spoonful of berries.

5. Place on a serving platter and serve immediately.

Nutrition: Calories 458, total fat 21 g, carb 60 g, Protein 18.1 g, sodium 905 mg

91.   Coconut Mandarin Cake

Preparation time: 10 minutes

Cooking time: 20 minutes

Servings: 3

Ingredients:

- ½ bag of shredded coconut
- 1 yellow or white cake mixed as directed
- 1 can drain mandarin oranges
- 1 cup brown sugar
- 1 stick of butter

Directions:

1. Place a parchment circle in a Dutch oven at the bottom of a 1-2. Spread the coconut out.

2. Place the mandarin oranges in any cute pattern on top of the coconut. Spread the top of the brown sugar.

3. Cut butter pats and put over brown sugar evenly. And scatter over the top of the mixed cake.

4. Put another ring on the lid (18-19) on a ring of coals (1 1-2). Cook for about 35-40 min until the cake is baked. Take off the heat. Clear the heat from the end. Let stand for 5 minutes or so. Then turn on a tray. Makes a minimum of 16 slices.

Nutrition: Calories 118, total fat 11 g, carb 65 g, Protein 18.1 g, sodium 155 mg

92.   Gingered Chocolate Bark

Preparation time: 15 minutes

Cooking time: 60 minutes

Servings: 8

Ingredients:

- 5 cups dark chocolate pieces
- 1 cup candied ginger, chopped into small pieces
- 1 cup pistachios, chopped

Directions

1. Line a baking sheet with parchment paper.
2. In a double boiler, melt the chocolate to a smooth consistency. Add in the ginger and stir well.
3. Spread the chocolate out in an even layer onto the parchment paper. Smooth with a spatula.
4. Sprinkle with chopped pistachios and allow to cool until hardened.
5. Break into small pieces before serving.

Nutrition:

Calories 145, total fat 43 g, carb 14 g, Protein 10.1 g, sodium 396 mg

93. Rich Brioche Pudding

Preparation time: 10 minutes

Cooking time: 50 minutes

Servings: 4

Ingredients:

- 5 cups day-old brioche, cubed
- 4 cups heavy cream
- 1 orange, juiced and zested
- 1½ cup brown sugar
- 9 eggs

Directions

1. Preheat oven to 375°F191°C.

2. Begin by cracking and separating the eggs. Leave three eggs whole and save only the yolks out of the remaining six. Whisk the whole eggs and the egg yolks together.

3. In a saucepan over medium heat, combine the heavy cream, ½ cup orange juice, 1 tablespoon orange zest, and brown sugar. Cook, stirring for 3-4 minutes.

4. Very slowly, incorporate the cream mixture into the eggs, whisking constantly to prevent cooking.

5. Place the brioche cubes in a large bowl and add the custard mixture. Toss to coat.

6. Transfer to a lightly oiled 9"x9" baking dish and place in the oven.

7. Bake for 40 minutes or until golden brown and hot, but still soft on the inside.

8. Serve warm or chilled.

Nutrition:

Calories 245, total fat 32 g, carb 57 g, Protein 10.1 g, sodium 126 mg

94.   Corn and Corn Fritters

Preparation time: 10 minutes

Cooking time: 35 minutes

Servings: 3

Ingredients:

- 2 Cups Corn Bread Mix
- ½ Cup Water
- ½ Cup Canned Corn, Rinsed and Drained
- 2 Tablespoons Sugar
- ¼ Cup butter

Directions:

1. This delicious food is great for breakfast, lunch, dinner, or just a snack. Attach the mixture of cornbread and sugar and combine it in a pan. Then slowly add the water and continue to blend.

2. While you want daily mixing, you don't want to over-mix. Next, add the drained Canned Corn and add a different mix.

3. The trick to making Fritters is to make sure the Cooking Oil is superhot when we start. Start with your Dutch oven and add some oil to cover the bottom, it is likely to be about 1-fifth of Cooking Oil's quarter cup. Place some of the batters in the oil and cook until crispy at the bottom for about 3 minutes.

4. Then flip and also cook over for another 3 minutes. Drain them as the remainder of the batter is out on paper towels.

Nutrition:

Calories 238, total fat 23.2 g, carb 30 g, Protein 11 g, sodium 456mg

95.   Bacon and Cheddar Cheese

Preparation time: 10 minutes

Cooking time: 35 minutes

Servings: 3

Ingredients:

- 14 dinner rolls (let them thaw first),
- About ten pieces of cooked bacon (break them into little pieces)
- ¼ cup of melted butter
- Topping
- 2 cups of cheddar cheese, grated

Directions

1. Cut each dinner roll in half, and then roll them in the butter until they are well coated. Arrange the butter-coated rolls in the Dutch oven. Sprinkle the mixture with bacon and cheese.

2. Cover the lid and let the dough rise slowly. Set the temperature of the Dutch oven to 350 °F and bake the mixture for 30 minutes. You can now serve for breakfast or eat later during the day.

Nutrition:

Calories 431, total fat 19.2 g, carb 90 g, Protein 6 g, sodium 784 mg

96.   Pot Fettuccine Alfredo Recipe

Preparation time: 10 minutes

Cooking time: 30 minutes

Servings: 3

Ingredients:

- 8 oz. Barilla Fettuccine Noodles
- 1 1/4 cup Shredded Parmesan Cheese
- 1 cup Heavy Whipping Cream
- 1/2 cup butter 1 stick, sliced thinly
- 3 cups Swanson Chicken Broth

Directions;

1. Bring three cups of Chicken Broth to boil at Med / High heat in 5–6 quarters Dutch Oven.

2. Breakin half the fettuccine noodles and add to the boiling broth.

3. For 1-2 minutes, cook Fettuccine, stirring frequently.

4. Decrease the heat to medium and remove any Pot Chicken Broth waste. {I used a large spoon to remove the extra Broth immediately} Stir in cream, butter, and garlic powder and parmesan cheese.

5. Leave for 5 minutes continuously or until the cheese is completely melted.

6. Serve Immediately.

Nutrition: Calories 341, total fat 12 g, carb 34 g, Protein 16 g, sodium 184 mg

97.   Chocolate Butterfinger Cake

Preparation Time: 10 minutes

Cooking Time: 30 minutes

Servings: 3

Ingredients:

- 1 chocolate cake mix
- 1 large Butterfinger candy bar broken in pieces
- 1 can sweeten condensed milk
- Nuts and ice cream
- 1 small jar Butterscotch topping

Directions:

1. Mix the cake according to the instructions and bake for 40 minutes or until the cake is finished at 350 ° or in a 1-2 Dutch oven.

2. Remove sweetened condensed milk and butterscotch over the cake when the cake is still dry. Sprinkle with the piece of chocolate. With nuts, ice cream, or whipped cream, serve warm.

Nutrition:

Calories 541, total fat 18 g, carb 81 g, Protein 12 g, sodium 123 mg

98.   Apple Dump Cake

Preparation time: 10 minutes

Cooking time: 30 minutes

Servings: 3

Ingredients:

- 1 cup (2 sticks) butter
- 1 cup pecans; chopped
- 1 pkg. butter pecan cake mix
- 1/4 cup brown sugar
- 2 cans apple pie filling

Directions

1. In an 11-inch Dutch oven, proceed to dump 2 cans of apple filling.

2. Sprinkle the sugar on top and then add the cake mix and the pecans but do not stir.

3. Thinly slice the butter and spread it on top.

4. Bake at 350 for 45-60 minutes.

Nutrition:

Calories 221, total fat 32 g, carb 12 g, Protein 21 g, sodium 290 mg

99.   Dutch Oven Brownie

Preparation time: 10 minutes

Cooking time: 50 minutes

Servings: 3

Ingredients:

- ½ cup canola or vegetable oil
- 3 tablespoons water
- 2 eggs
- 1 cup m&m baking bits (3/4 cup for batter + ¼ cup for topping)
- 18.3 oz. Betty crocker fudge brownie mix {1 box}

Directions

1. Preheat your oven to 325 degrees F.
2. Once done, lightly grease a 10-inch Dutch oven.
3. In a bowl, mix together the eggs, Brownie Mix, oil, water and 3/4 cup M&M Baking Bits.
4. Carefully spread the mixture into your Dutch oven.
5. Bake for 40 minutes. Once the time is up, remove from oven and evenly spread the remaining 1/4 cup of M&M Baking Bits on top.
6. Return to oven and bake for 10 minutes more or until done.

7. Once done, let the Dutch oven cool on the wire rack for some minutes and then use a plastic knife to slice the Brownie.

8. Serve and enjoy. You can serve with vanilla ice cream if you wish.

Nutrition:

Calories 234, total fat 10 g, carb 32 g, Protein 12 g, sodium 842 mg

100.   Strawberry Cobbler

Preparation time: 10 minutes

Cooking time: 50 minutes

Servings: 3

Ingredients:

- 3 tablespoons butter, melted
- 1 stick butter {1/2 cup}, melted
- Philadelphia whipped cream cheese {8 oz.}
- 2 cans of strawberry pie filling {21 oz. Each}
- 1 box (15.25 oz.) Betty Crocker French vanilla cake mix

Directions

1. Preheat your oven to 350 degrees.

2. Place 1/2 stick of melted butter into the bottom of a 12-inch Dutch oven. Swirl the butter around to coat the Dutch oven evenly.

3. Once done, dump both cans of strawberry pie filling inside and use a wooden spoon to spread out evenly.

4. Spread dollops of cream cheese on top of the pie filling.

5. In a bowl, mix together the remaining 1 stick of melted butter and the Cake Mix. Use a spoon or your fingers to break up the chunks.

6. Spread the mixture on top of the cream cheese dollops and pie filling.

7. Bake for 50 minutes. The top should be crispy and the edges hot and bubbly.

8. Remove and serve with vanilla ice cream if you wish.

Nutrition:

Calories 214, total fat 23 g, carb 21 g, Protein 21 g, sodium 287 mg

101.   Blueberry Dump Cake

Preparation time: 10 minutes

Cooking time: 40 minutes

Servings: 3

Ingredients:

- 1-pint blueberries
- 1/2 cup butter (1 stick or you could use margarine)
- 1 cup milk (you can use skim or you could use almond milk or other dairy free milk in place of regular milk)
- 1 cup sugar
- 1 cup flour (all-purpose or whole wheat pastry flour)

Directions

1. Preheat your oven to 375 and spray your Dutch oven with cooking spray or spread a bit of butter in it and set aside.

2. Melt the butter. You can melt it for 30 seconds in the microwave. In a bowl, combine the butter, flour, milk and sugar. Mix well and then pour into the prepared Dutch oven.

3. Spread the blueberries on top and then bake for 40-45 minutes. The edges should start to brown.

4. Remove from the oven and let it cool for 10 minutes.

5. Serve.

Nutrition: Calories 201, total fat 23 g, carb 12 g, Protein 13 g, sodium 732 mg

102.   Heavenly Peach Cobbler

Preparation time: 10 minutes

Cooking time: 20 minutes

Servings: 3

Ingredients:

- ½ pack vanilla cake mix
- 1 cup lemon-lime soda (Sprite/7 Up)
- 4 cups fruit (peaches, apples, berries, etc.)
- 2 tablespoons unsalted butter, cold, diced
- Whipped cream

Directions

1. Lightly grease the Dutch oven with cooking spray.
2. Add the cake mix and soda to a mixing bowl. Mix well to make a thick batter.
3. Arrange the fruit in the Dutch oven; pour the batter over it.
4. Top with the diced butter and sugar.
5. Heat the Dutch oven to 350°F (175°C).
6. Cover and cook for 20 minutes until the top is golden brown and the juices are bubbling.
7. Serve warm with whipped cream.

Nutrition: Calories 282, Fat 6 g, carbs 57 g, Protein 3 g, sodium 304 mg

103.   Cherry Clafouti

Preparation time: 10 minutes

Cooking time: 30 minutes

Servings: 3

Ingredients:

- ¾ pound fresh or frozen and thawed cherries stemmed and pitted
- 2 large eggs
- ¼ cup of sugar
- ½ cup whole milk
- 1 teaspoon vanilla extract
- ½ cup all-purpose flour

Directions

1. Preheat the Dutch oven to 400°F (200°C). Evenly spread butter to cover the inside surface.

2. Spread the cherries over the bottom.

3. Whisk the eggs in a bowl. Add the sugar. Mix until well blended and frothy.

4. Add the flour, milk, and vanilla to another mixing bowl. Mix well.

5. Combine the mixtures to make a smooth batter.

6. Pour the batter over the cherries.

7. Cook, uncovered, for 30 minutes until the top is golden brown. Check by inserting a toothpick; it should come out clean. If not, cook for a few more minutes.

8. Serve warm.

Nutrition

Calories 92, Fat 2 g, carbs 16 g, Protein 3 g, sodium 26 mg

104.   Pecan Pralines

Preparation time: 10 minutes

Cooking time: 20 minutes

Servings: 3

Ingredients:

- 1 cup whipping cream
- 3 cups light brown sugar
- ¼ cup butter
- 2 tablespoons corn syrup
- 1 teaspoon vanilla extract

Directions

1. Preheat the Dutch oven to 350°F (175°C).

2. Spread the pecan halves in the Dutch oven and cook for 5 minutes. Stir-cook for another 5 minutes. Set aside.

3. Clean the Dutch oven and add the whipping cream, brown sugar, butter, and corn syrup.

4. Boil over high heat for 4–6 minutes until the sugar melts completely, stirring occasionally.

5. Remove from heat and add the pecans and vanilla; stir for 1–2 minutes. Let cool for a while.

6. Place a spoonful of the mixture on a wax paper; allow to firm up for 10–15 minutes.

7. Serve warm.

Nutrition

Calories 228, Fat 14 g, carbs 25 g, Protein 2 g, sodium 31 mg

105.   Quick and Easy Pop Brownies

Preparation time: 10 minutes

Cooking time: 45 minutes

Servings: 3

Ingredients:

- 1 box brownie mix
- 1 can soda pop
- ¾ pound chocolate chips

Directions

1. Line the Dutch oven with parchment paper.

2. Add the brownie mix and soda to a mixing bowl. Mix well until you get a smooth mixture.

3. Pour the batter over the parchment paper. Sprinkle the chocolate chips on top.

4. Heat to 350°F (175°C) and bake for 45–60 minutes until well set. Check by inserting a toothpick; it should come out clean. If not, cook for a few more minutes.

5. Slice and serve warm.

Nutrition

Calories 241, Fat 13 g, carbs 35 g, Protein 2 g, sodium 16 mg

106.   Chocolate Chip Cookies

Preparation time: 10 minutes

Cooking time: 30 minutes

Servings: 3

Ingredients:

- 1 cup butter, softened
- ¾ cup packed brown sugar
- 1 egg
- 1 teaspoon baking soda
- 2¼ cups flour

Directions

1. Add the butter-sugar to a mixing bowl. Mix well.

2. Beat the eggs in another bowl. Mix well.

3. Add the sea salt, baking soda, and flour; mix again.

4. Combine the mixtures until smooth.

5. Divide into 24 balls.

6. Line the Dutch oven with parchment paper and lightly grease it with cooking spray.

7. Arrange the balls on the bottom.

8. Cover and cook for 6 minutes. If cookies have turned light brown, take them out. If not, cook for 2–4 more minutes. Do not overcook.

9. Let cool for a while.

10. Serve warm.

Nutrition

Calories 220, Fat 11 g, carbs 29 g, Protein 2 g, sodium 100 mg

107.   Dutch Oven Brownies

Preparation time: 10 minutes

Cooking time: 40 minutes

Servings: 3

Ingredients:

- 1 box brownie mix
- ½ cup melted butter
- 2 large eggs
- 1 cup of chocolate chips
- 1 teaspoon vanilla extract

Directions

1. Add the brownie mix to a large mixing bowl and stir in the melted butter, eggs, and water, and chocolate chips until just combined, being careful not to over-mix the batter.

2. Line the Dutch oven with a piece of parchment paper and pour in the brownie mixture.

3. Bake at 350°F (180°C) for 25–30 minutes.

4. Let the brownies cool slightly and then cut into squares and serve.

Nutrition

Calories 502, Fat 27 g, carbs 63.2 g, Protein 5.7 g, sodium 308 mg

108.   Double Chocolate Cake

Preparation time: 10 minutes

Cooking time: 40 minutes

Servings: 3

Ingredients:

- 1 box chocolate cake mix
- ¼ cup whole milk
- 1 cup of chocolate chips
- 2 cups heavy whipping cream
- 3 tablespoons powdered sugar

Directions

1. Add the cake mix to a large mixing bowl and stir in the milk and chocolate chips until just combined, being careful not to over-mix the batter.

2. Line the Dutch oven with a piece of parchment paper and pour in the chocolate cake mixture.

3. Bake at 350°F (180°C) for about 30 minutes.

4. Remove the cake from the Dutch oven and place it on a cooling rack. Let it cool completely.

5. Add the whipping cream, powdered sugar, and vanilla extract to a large mixing bowl and beat with a hand mixer.

6. Cut the chocolate cake in half to create two layers. Spread half of the whipped cream on one layer, cover

with the second layer, and decorate the whole cake with whipped cream.

7. If desired, sprinkle with more chocolate chips for better presentation.

Nutrition

Calories 594, Fat 36.9 g, carbs 64.5 g, Protein 6.3 g, sodium 572 mg

Conclusion

When it comes to preparing food while camping, there are many things to consider. For example, some campers choose to bring their lighted gas stoves or grills while others just choose to use the same one that they used at home

Camping is an ideal way to enjoy fantastic local produce. The best food and drink for camping involves various things to different individuals (and differs widely based on whether you are camping in a vehicle or backpacking). Picnics and camping are generally a bit better, since if it's already done, you're only transporting it, but preparing a great meal. In contrast, camping is not that challenging, as long as you meet certain general instructions. Probably your home kitchen has a freezer, pantry, sufficient cabinets, and quick access to a nearby supermarket where thousands of choices are accessible for any meal. However, the camping kitchen of yours is a little more mounted down, perhaps limited to a cooler, storage box, plastic jar/container or two, and perhaps a weekend bag made of paper that remains in your car's backseat.

The natural wood smoke gives any dish an amazing taste, while the gentle crackle of flames enables campfire cooking a relaxing way to experience the great outdoors. However, you don't have to associate fewer ingredients on hand with dull recipes, especially when you realize how some main staples will blend in dozens of ways, if not hundreds, enabling you to cook up dishes to please a lonely hiker, a romantic couple, a starving family, as well as a whole crowd sitting across the campfire.

It is probably better to make all food planning you can do as minimal as possible while camping. Minimize the use of perishable food products and follow the proper sanitation precautions to ensure your group members' welfare. However, that picnic and cookouts are a feature of the camping culture. For this purpose, it is important to take care of all the precautions. There are a few food planning staples that you shouldn't skip, regardless of whether you intend to prepare for your upcoming camping trip or hiking. A case of matches and some fluid used as a firelighter are first and foremost.

The majority tend to cook over an outdoor fire at their campsite, so you'd be not so lucky without the need for a means to start one. For the dishes, a medium-sized to large-sized lightweight bowl, a similar size skillet, foil of aluminum, and a compact grill that can be put over a fire grate are the real necessities. This variation of cooking appliances helps produce Ham, eggs, lentils, and pasta. Finally, don't skip your spatula and tongs. It's far from enjoyable to pull food from a bare-handed fire.